T0271100

The Emptiness of Business Excellence

In Search of Excellence was the book that launched a thousand popular management books. In this concise book, David and Jack Collins demonstrate the emptiness of business excellence and in so doing reveal the flawed foundations of popular management theory.

Focusing upon the conduct of those organizations vaunted as 'exemplars of excellence' the authors build upon insightful case reports to demonstrate wholesale misconduct at the very heart of the excellence project. Indeed, *The Emptiness of Business Excellence* demonstrates that the exemplars of excellence indulged bribery, corruption, racism, sexism and anti-Semitism . . . and more besides! Furthermore, the book demonstrates that, despite their claims to knowledge, Peters and Waterman often knew little about the financial performance of their excellent organizations and were either unaware of or had chosen to overlook reports which highlighted deeply problematic conduct within those formations, which they offered as beacons for change and renewal.

This book will be of interest to researchers, scholars and students with an interest in business and management, especially those focusing on the realities of managerial practice.

David Collins is Professor in Management at Northumbria University, UK and Visiting Professor in Management at the University of the Faroe Islands.

Jack Collins is a student within the School of History, Classics and Archaeology at the University of Newcastle-upon-Tyne, UK.

Routledge Focus on Business and Management

The fields of business and management have grown exponentially as areas of research and education. This growth presents challenges for readers trying to keep up with the latest important insights. *Routledge Focus on Business and Management* presents small books on big topics and how they intersect with the world of business research.

Individually, each title in the series provides coverage of a key academic topic, whilst collectively, the series forms a comprehensive collection across the business disciplines.

Work Organizational Reforms and Employment Relations in the Automotive Industry
American Employment Relations in Transition
Kenichi Shinohara

Qualitative Management Research in Context
Data Collection, Interpretation and Narrative
Edited by Bruno Américo, Stewart Clegg and César Tureta

Marx in Management and Organisation Studies
Rethinking Value, Labour and Class Struggles
Frederick Harry Pitts

The Emptiness of Business Excellence
The Flawed Foundations of Popular Management Theory
David Collins and Jack Collins

The Innovative Management Education Ecosystem
Reskilling and Upskilling the Future Workforce
Jordi Diaz, Daphne Halkias and Paul W. Thurman

For more information about this series, please visit: www.routledge.com/Routledge-Focus-on-Business-and-Management/book-series/FBM

The Emptiness of Business Excellence

Business Excellence

The Flawed Foundations of Popular Management Theory

David Collins and Jack Collins

Routledge
Taylor & Francis Group

LONDON AND NEW YORK

First published 2023
by Routledge
4 Park Square, Milton Park, Abingdon, Oxon OX14 4RN

and by Routledge
605 Third Avenue, New York, NY 10158

Routledge is an imprint of the Taylor & Francis Group, an informa business

British Library Cataloguing-in-Publication Data
A catalogue record for this book is available from the British Library

ISBN: 978-1-032-37623-3 (hbk)
ISBN: 978-1-032-37624-0 (pbk)
ISBN: 978-1-003-34108-6 (ebk)

DOI: 10.4324/9781003341086

Typeset in Times New Roman
by Apex CoVantage, LLC

Contents

1 Introduction

The Enduring Significance of
In Search of Excellence

On October 15 1982, Tom Peters and Robert Waterman (1982) published *In Search of Excellence*.[1] This book has, Kiechel (2010) suggests, become iconic. It offers, he advises, perhaps the closest thing that the field of management studies has to an overarching organizing paradigm.

The book you now hold in your hands has been timed to coincide with the 40th anniversary of the first publication of this iconic text. It has been designed to offer an historical account of the development of *In Search of Excellence*. In addition it has been arranged to offer a distinctive, critical review of its core claims, orientations and, perhaps uniquely, its practices. Going beyond the limitations of conventional critiques (see Chapter 2), which focus upon excellence *in theory*, this book will offer critical reflections on *the practice* of business excellence and upon the lived experience of those who have toiled within the (so-called) exemplars of business excellence. These reflections on the practice of business excellence, as we shall see, demonstrate, both, the emptiness of the excellence project and the flawed foundations that it laid for popular management theory.

This introductory chapter has been designed to preface our core concerns. It will demonstrate the reach and significance of *In Search of Excellence* so that readers will understand why it is vital that we understand the core philosophy advanced by Peters and Waterman in 1982 and the legacy of their iconic text.

* * * * *

In Search of Excellence was written by two, largely anonymous management consultants – Tom Peters and Robert (Bob) Waterman – who met while working for and McKinsey Co. during the 1970s. By the mid-1980s however this publication had transformed the lives of its authors. Indeed by 1985 Tom Peters and Bob Waterman were famous: in demand and indeed widely feted as 'gurus' of management (see Collins, 2021). Today Peters

DOI: 10.4324/9781003341086-1

and Waterman are, we accept, perhaps less well known. Some of those who currently enjoy the title of 'manager' and indeed some students currently studying for a qualification in 'management' may well be blissfully unaware of the manner in which Tom Peters and Bob Waterman have shaped their lives and their professional endeavours. Fame, after all, is often fleeting and the world of celebrity is nothing if not fickle. Yet it would be a mistake to suggest that any current absence of recognition makes the names Peters and Waterman somehow irrelevant to the history of management studies and/ or the contemporary concerns and processes of managerial work. In this introductory chapter, we will demonstrate that *In Search of Excellence* was famous, remains iconic and deserves, now, to be remembered because, even though you may not realize it, Peters and Waterman have changed, quite profoundly, the manner in which we understand the very nature of managerial work.

We recognize, of course, that not all would be inclined to offer Peters and Waterman this elevated position in the pantheon of management studies. Indeed many, as we shall see, plainly consider Peters and Waterman to be *infamous* and would insist that their contribution to the field of management studies while widely known in the 1980s is now best forgotten. Acknowledging that the mere mention of *In Search of Excellence* tends to excite and to polarize opinion (at least among those who can recall the 1980s), this book offers a critical review of this text and a distinctive reappraisal of its legacy. We begin therefore with reflections on the development of *In Search of Excellence* and on its unlikely and unexpected success!

An Unlikely Success

In Search of Excellence was first published in the middle of a deep economic recession: the worst that Americans had experienced in a generation. Commentators generally accept that this recession was pivotal to the success of *In Search of Excellence* and indeed to the success of the excellence project as a whole (see for example Saunders and Wong, 1985: Kauffman 1993; Byrne, 2001; Bogner, 2002). Yet even before this economic downturn many within the US had voiced fears concerning America's standing in the world (Hayes and Abernathy, 1980) and its faltering performance in the face of competition from Japan (see Kahn, 1970; Kahn and Pepper, 1978). *In Search of Excellence* clearly reflected these concerns but, unlike some other contemporary accounts (see Pascale and Athos [1981] 1986), it did not offer a simple counsel of despair. Instead it deliberately and self-consciously projected the argument advanced by Ronald Reagan[2] (among others) that a great national crusade to 'make America great again' was not only necessary but entirely possible.[3]

Despite this context and, indeed despite the pedigree of its broader political and economic discourse, the publishers of *In Search of Excellence* had, it seems, very modest expectations for their product and for good reason. In the 1970s the general public had, beyond the occasional corporate scandal, literally no interest in reading books on the business of management (see Collins, 2013, 2021). Crainer (1997), a former employee of the *Tom Peters Company* (the training and consulting organization established to market the wares of Tom Peters[4]), suggests that the publishers – *Harper and Row* – were keenly aware that books on the business of management had very limited commercial potential in this period. He observes that *Harper and Row* forecast total sales of between 10,000 and 20,000 copies, and so, settled upon an initial print run of just 15,000 copies. Tom Peters (2018) however remembers things differently. He confides that *Harper and Row* did not actually believe that *In Search of Excellence* had any serious commercial potential *at all* and had, in fact, commissioned a print run of just 5,000 copies. To the surprise of all those concerned,[5] however, *In Search of Excellence* quickly proved itself to be a runaway, commercial success.

The complexities of international publishing agreements and the presence of unlicensed *ersatz* editions in territories such as China (see Crainer, 1997), for example, make it rather difficult to form reliable estimations of the overall book sales enjoyed by Peters and Waterman (1982). Nonetheless, it is clear that, despite the publisher's dismal forecast, some three million copies of *In Search of Excellence* were sold between late 1982 and the middle of this turbulent decade (see Saunders and Wong, 1985).[6] Indeed Peters and Waterman (1982) held the number one slot on *The New York Times* best-sellers listings continuously for two years (Collins, 2000) and were displaced from the number one position, slipping to number two, only when the lead author, working with Nancy Austin released *A Passion for Excellence* (Peters and Austin, 1985).

The Ohio College Library Centre (OCLC[7]), a non-profit co-operative organization established to improve public access to information, began compiling lists of US library holdings in 1989. It reports that *In Search of Excellence* was the most widely held monograph in that year. Indeed data compiled by the OCLC demonstrates that *In Search of Excellence* remained the most widely-held monograph in US library collections until at least 1997.[8]

Contemporary estimations of overall sales published by the *Tom Peters Group*[9] while prone to under-reporting, suggest that perhaps ten million copies of *In Search of Excellence* have now been sold. Recognizing both the commercial success of this book and the enduring appeal of its core message, the publisher *Bloomsbury* named *In Search of Excellence* 'The Greatest Business Book of All Time' (see Collins, 2007). However, not all are content to announce the end of history.[10] Indeed there are many who have attempted to (re)write the history of the excellence project in order to reveal the ways in which the central *conceit* of *In Search of Excellence* is undone by a whole host of conceptual, methodological and empirical failings. Many of these critiques as we shall see in our next chapter are accurate and well-made: *In Search of Excellence* is, in academic terms, a deeply flawed study with foundations that tend to buckle under the weight of the authors' core claims. Yet, the excellence project has proven itself to be largely immune to academic critique. Indeed it has done much to shape our understanding of business and our appreciation of the management process. Truthfully *In Search of Excellence* has altered *quite fundamentally* the manner in which we now think about, talk about, and when all is said and done, practice the art of management. *In Search of Excellence* is, frankly, the prototype that became the archetype for the billion dollar industry known variously as 'popular management' (see Rosner, 2000; Collins, 2021), Heathrow Organization Theory and/ or Handy Pocket Theory (see Burrell, 1997).

This little book, published to coincide with the 40th anniversary of the first publication of *In Search of Excellence*, has been designed to offer a timely (re)appraisal of this iconic text. Our reappraisal will reveal the hollow core of the excellence project *and* the flawed foundations of popular management. Yet, we reject the siren calls of debunking, which suggest that *In Search of Excellence* is somehow trivial and unworthy of sustained scrutiny (see Collins, 2001). Instead we proceed from the understanding that *In Search of Excellence* is a deeply flawed work, which remains nonetheless hugely significant and worthy of serious and sustained academic analysis. Indeed we will insist that *In Search of Excellence* must be taken seriously as a defining influence on the landscape of management thought and practice. Yet, we have no desire to construct ourselves as apologists for the excellence project. To be clear: as an intellectual exercise the excellence project *is* largely beyond redemption. Our intention on the eve of the 40th anniversary of the first publication of *In Search of Excellence* is, therefore, to offer a robust and informed critique of this text, which recognizes the nature and appeal of the excellence project *and yet* challenges, productively, its central *conceit*. To this end and, perhaps for the first time in this context, we will shine a light on the practices of the excellent organization and on the lived experience of those who have worked within these formations.

Accordingly, the analysis of *In Search of Excellence* developed between these covers returns to the very foundations of the project to offer, what might be termed, an archaeological excavation of business excellence. Focusing upon the 14 organizations, highlighted as beacons of best practice (see Chapter 2), we will examine the extent to which those corporate entities celebrated within the covers of *In Search of Excellence* were

a) actually known to the authors and b) truly driven by the eight attributes said to underpin the organizational practices necessary for 'excellence.' We will argue that Peters and Waterman have placed exclamation marks within their analysis where questions marks are merited.[11] Indeed we will demonstrate that at least some of those corporations vaunted as 'exemplars of excellence' were, in this period, highly secretive and produced no useful data on their business performance that could have supported the ambition of the authors. Furthermore, we will argue that Peters and Waterman turned a blind eye to the practices evident within their excellent organizations, and in so doing, ignored contemporary reports which demonstrated that their exemplars of excellence were, in fact, often engaged in activities that were simply venal and often criminal.

To facilitate this re-view and reappraisal our monograph will set to one side those conventional academic critiques that have tried and failed to unsettle the foundations of excellence project to offer a new analysis that reveals the *real politic* of business and through this the lived experience of business excellence. Our book, therefore, is structured as follows: Chapter two offers, necessarily, a critical analysis and review of *In Search of Excellence* (Peters and Waterman, 1982). While conceding that the excellence project has continued to evolve over the past 40 years (see Collins, 2000, 2007, 2022), we will focus upon the manner in which the authors came to constitute the essential architecture of business excellence.[12] Building upon this account of excellence 'in theory' we will review a selection of the key criticisms voiced in opposition to *In Search of Excellence*. While acknowledging that these critiques are, for the most part, accurate and well-made, we will suggest that conventional forms of academic criticism, too often, misunderstand this endeavour. Indeed we will argue that, too often, critics of *In Search of Excellence* miss the point of the excellence project, and so, misunderstand its core appeal. Countering the arguments that underpin conventional forms of academic critique, therefore, we will argue that the excellence project exists not to catalogue the managerial world but to engineer a change in its essence. In this regard the extent to which Peters and Waterman offer an account of the business of management that is reliable and/ or representative in some statistical sense is largely irrelevant. Thus, we will argue that the excellence project needs to be read as a species of evangelism (see Boltanski and Chiapello, 2007) designed to secure consent for, if not commitment to, a larger project of socio-economic change; a world where the customer is King, where change is the norm, and any commitment to pluralism is waved away as a nostalgic affectation unsuited to the contemporary *needs* of business.

Chapter three will shift focus from theory to practice as we consider the lived experience of business excellence. This chapter will draw upon newspaper archives and other published sources to invite a reconsideration of the ways and means of business excellence. It will offer answers to a simple, obvious yet largely unanswered question: is the theoretical account of business excellence developed by Peters and Waterman (1982) actually congruent with the business practices reported during this period?

Providing answers to this important question Chapter three will offer, in effect, 14 brief case studies, designed to excavate the business practices of those organizations said to constitute the exemplars of excellence. As we shall see, our excavations uncover uncomfortable truths about the reality of corporate conduct within those formations said to typify best practice. Indeed, where Peters and Waterman (1982) invite us to view the excellent organizations as models of probity and beacons for good practice, our 'excavations' uncover a different reality; a world underscored by bribery, corruption, false accounting, money laundering, racism, sexism, anti-unionism and anti-Semitism! Finally Chapter four will offer a summary of our analysis and concluding comments. These concluding comments, as we shall see, have been designed to cement a new appreciation of the excellent project within academia and within those communities which have, knowingly or otherwise, accepted *In Search of Excellence* as a practical guide for their leadership endeavours.

Notes

1 This is the date of publication offered by Peters (2001a).
2 Reagan advanced this position throughout the campaign which saw him secure the American presidency in 1980.
3 Crainer (1997) suggests that Pascale and Athos ([1981] 1986) offered Americans only humble pie, whereas Peters and Waterman (1982) offered mom and apple pie.
4 See tompeterscompany.com
5 Collins (2022) observes that while Robert Waterman had no contractual rights to the proceeds of *In Search of Excellence,* Peters' former employees, *McKinsey and Co* did. Indeed thanks to the intervention and support of Bob Waterman, *McKinsey* had agreed that Peters would exit 'the firm' with a financial settlement on the understanding that *McKinsey* would share equally in the royalties earned on the first 50,000 sales of *In Search of Excellence.* Given the publisher's expectations as to sales, this was of course a very generous settlement.
6 Byrne (2001) is one of those who struggles with the estimation of sales data in this context. He suggests that *In Search of Excellence* eventually sold more than three million copies, whereas the data produced by the OCLC (see footnote vii) and Saunders and Wong (1985) suggests that this sales figure was achieved promptly and certainly no later than 1986.
7 See oclc.org for an overview of the work of this co-operative.
8 We suspect that *In Search of Excellence* continues to be amongst the most widely held monographs within US libraries. However, since the OCLC has now changed its approach and no longer uses 'monographs' as an organizing category, it is difficult to substantiate this claim. That said the 'top 1000' list

published in 2007 (see oclc.org/research/top1000/complete.html) lists *In Search of Excellence* – during the year of the 25th anniversary of its first publication – at number 451. This, it may be interesting to note, places Peters and Waterman (1982) between 'The Little Engine that Could' and a text designed to outline American library cataloguing conventions.

9 This claim appears on the web-site of The Tom Peters Group, which may be found at: tompeterscompany.com

10 This is of course a nod towards the work of Fukuyama (1992) and the critiques that arose in the light of his analysis.

11 Tom Peters uses a red exclamation mark as a component of his branded identity.

12 Pascale and Athos ([1981] 1986) and Collins (2022) concede that others, within and beyond McKinsey, contributed to the very foundations of the excellence project. In chapter two we will acknowledge the presence of this larger network. However, we will less positively also suggest that to call this activity 'research' is to misrepresent what would soon be revealed as an *ad hoc* collection of, often brief, organizational encounters.

2 *In Search of Excellence* in Theory

Introduction

This chapter considers business excellence 'in theory.' It will build upon the analyses developed in Collins (2000, 2007, 2008, 2022) to offer reflections on the manner in which *In Search of Excellence* constitutes its core orientations. In addition, this chapter will offer an account of the development of the 7-S framework that, as we shall see, underpins the very foundations of the excellence project. In this regard, our approach is genuinely distinctive.

Most texts prepared for students and indeed for practitioners of 'management' seem content merely to exhibit the building blocks of the excellence project. For example, textbooks on 'management' (and the crib guides that populate that segment of the internet concerned with the business of management) generally volunteer the fact that the excellence project demands that managers secure an appropriate balance between the 'hard' and the 'soft' elements of organization. Furthermore these texts (and crib guides) tend to suggest that *In Search of Excellence* represents a significant contribution to the field of management studies because it demonstrates that excellence in business flows from *and is characterized by* a commitment to eight core organizational attributes. Yet, while these textbook accounts provide an exposition of the outline manifesto developed by Peters and Waterman (1982), they do not consider the labour required to erect the edifice of the excellence project. As a result, textbook treatments of *In Search of Excellence* tend to lack both historical context and critical intent. In this regard, management textbooks (and on-line crib-sheets) offer 'ready-made' (Latour, 1987) accounts of human endeavour. These 'ready-made' accounts are problematic, however, because they elide the contests and controversies that surround the development of the excellence project and in so doing, treat the core claims of *In Search of Excellence* as simple *findings*. In this chapter, we choose a different path. While this chapter must, of course, offer an account of the architecture of the excellence project, we will argue that

DOI: 10.4324/9781003341086-2

it is important to look behind the project's façade in order to consider a) the problems that led to its construction and b) the (political) processes involved in its erection.

Accordingly, this chapter will offer a critical analysis of the constitution and construction of *In Search of Excellence*. It will, of course, describe the core components of business excellence and its core claims. Yet, in so doing, the chapter will track the more fundamental issues – ignored by 'ready-made' accounts – that led McKinsey and Co. to commission the research on 'organizational effectiveness,' which, as we shall see, provided the empirical foundations of *In Search of Excellence*.

We will begin with reflections on the development of the McKinsey 7-S framework. Having reflected upon the development of this now iconic framework, we will consider the manner in which this attempt to encapsulate the socio-technical totality of organizational life was translated into the eight core attributes, said to describe and to account for business excellence. We will discuss these attributes, while considering a range of the criticisms that have been raised against the core claims of *In Search of Excellence*. Many of these criticisms, as we will learn, are accurate and remain (in academic circles at least) pertinent. Yet, we will suggest that the work of Peters and Waterman (1982) remains largely immune to conventional forms of academic criticism. We will account for this paradoxical situation and in so doing we will conclude this chapter with the suggestion that there is now – on the eve of the 40th anniversary of the first publication of *In Search of Excellence* – the need for an alternative form of criticism designed to precipitate a fundamental reappraisal of the excellence project and its legacy.

The McKinsey 7-S Framework

This book has been timed to coincide with the anniversary of the first publication of *In Search of Excellence* on October 15, 1982 (Peters, 2001a). While this date is of course significant and *should* be observed it may be useful to remind ourselves that authors often live with projects for some years before their work is released to the general public. This book is, for example, scheduled for publication in late 2022. Yet, together we are toiling to produce this, the first draft of our reappraisal of the excellence project in October 2021. This declaration may come as a surprise to some readers because authors and publishers tend to efface the authorial labour – the early drafts, false starts, remedial work, proof-reading, fact-checking, indexing etc. – that is required to bring the finished project before you, the reader.

Tom Peters has managed and maintained a position at the head of 'popular management' now for some 40 years and has along the way published 18 books (and an assortment of pamphlets, blog posts and newspaper columns) on the business of management (Collins, 2021, 2022). Peters is, therefore, very well placed to lift the curtain on those processes of planning, writing and redrafting that, while they are part-and-parcel of authorship, are generally hidden from the public. In this respect it is useful to note that Peters dates the birth of the excellent project quite precisely *and* prior to October 1982. This is, of course, a refreshing acknowledgement of the protracted nature of the authorial process. Yet Peters' public acknowledgement of his authorial practice is slightly problematic and potentially confusing because at different times he has identified quite different birth dates for the excellence project.

In 1982 (Peters and Waterman, 1982: 12) Peters suggested that July 4, 1979 represents the true birth date of *In Search of Excellence*. This was he suggests the day when *Royal Dutch Shell* offered feedback on a presentation on 'excellence,' which demonstrated that there was within the wider business community an appetite for research designed to probe the nature of organizational effectiveness and the processes necessary to its delivery. More recently, however, Peters (2018: 30) has offered another birth date, which suggests that the excellence project is just a little older than previously acknowledged. This date is 'Good Friday 1978.' Elaborating on this moment in time Peters tells us:

> 'It was Easter week 1978. The main computer in the San Francisco office of McKinsey & Co., where I worked as a consultant, chose to crash 36 hours before our managing director was scheduled to give a report on an important project to the top team at Dart Industries in Los Angeles.
>
> With the computer down, his team was unable to prepare the sort of presentation he wished to make. I, meanwhile, was working frantically and independently on a project commissioned by the powers that be in the firm's New York headquarters. Though I was psyched by the project, it had the uninspiring title of "Improving Organizational Effectiveness." John Larson (the S. F. McKinsey boss) came to me in desperation (Dart was a core client) and said, in effect, "*Can you put something short but somewhat sweet together and fob it off on Dart and save my ass?*"
>
> "Sure," I said in a flash; one dreams of saving one's boss's ass, right? . . . I got home about 10:30 p.m. and, in a daze, dutifully went to my home office and started pulling material together for Dart. I honestly have no idea what next transpired, but I do know, Bic pen in hand . . . I crafted a draft cover page with but one word, in all capital letters: EXCELLENCE.'
>
> (28 original emphasis, capitalization, and parentheses)

The account of the genesis of the excellence project that is offered by Pascale and Athos [1981] (1986) is less concerned to identify an absolute point of origin. Instead it invites us to consider the development of the 7-S framework, which offered an analytical heuristic for the early stirrings on 'organizational effectiveness.'

Probing the processes of innovation that spawned the 7-S framework, Pascale and Athos suggest that this model was first developed to elaborate Peters' intuition as to the practices of effective organizations:

> Peters pointed out in a working paper on "excellent companies" that firms so designated explicitly managed a wider range of variables than other companies.
>
> (Pascale and Athos [1981] 1986: ix)

Yet while Pascale and Athos give due credit to Tom Peters they are keen to remind us that his working paper was actually developed to support a programme of applied research that McKinsey had commissioned. Commenting on the aims and scope of the research project instituted by McKinsey, Pascale and Athos ([1981] 1986: viii-ix) note that together, Peters and his colleague Jim Bennett had been instructed 'to review the entire literature and current thought about effectiveness.' Reflecting upon the working paper, which Peters developed as a response to this brief they note that he had

> concluded that the emphasis upon strategy and structure [which at that time characterised management practice and, indeed, the advice generated by the consulting industry] had gone beyond the point of diminishing returns, and that other factors were also critically important and deserved more attention.

Following the publication of this working paper, the senior management of McKinsey drafted Robert (Bob) Waterman to the team charged to investigate 'effectiveness.' Pascale and Athos ([1981] 1986: ix) observe that Waterman accepted the core concerns articulated by Peters but feared that these would be 'very difficult to convey persuasively to a wider audience of consultants and executives steeped in the strategy-structure emphasis [which McKinsey among other leading consulting organizations had so effectively promoted].' With the issue of communicability high on his personal agenda, Waterman, we are told, invited Athos (who had combined consultancy, research and graduate school teaching), to join the effectiveness team as a consultant. Soon afterwards a similar invitation was tendered to Pascale (thanks to his work on cross-cultural management). Explaining the factors underpinning the enlargement of the team, Pascale and Athos, tell us that Bob Waterman anticipated that their involvement would add conceptual sophistication and communicability to the outline prospectus that Peters and his colleague, Jim Bennett had begun to craft.

In June 1978, just as Waterman had hoped, Athos made a suggestion to this small collective that we might now view as highly significant. He suggested the need for a conceptual schema designed to organize the core variables identified by Peters and Bennett 'so that their interrelationships might be emphasized, and so that "fit" among the variables might be better understood' (Pascale and Athos [1981] 1986: ix). Arguing that an alliterative approach would improve learning within a population inclined to focus narrowly upon strategy and structure, Athos proposed a 5-S framework and persuaded Peters and Waterman to embrace this schema.

To facilitate the alliterative approach advocated by Athos, the collective was persuaded to substitute 'superordinate goals' for what had previously been labelled 'guiding concepts' and agreed, initially, on three 'hard s' factors (strategy, structure and systems) and two 'soft s' factors, namely, 'style' and 'superordinate goals.' Almost immediately, however, both Peters and Pascale independently suggested the need for an additional 's-factor,' which they duly labelled 'sequencing.' Therefore, by 1978, McKinsey and Co. had the bones of a 'six-s' framework.

Pascale and Athos concede that it was Bob Waterman who carried the torch for this 'six-s' framework within McKinsey, in part through the publication of a paper entitled 'Structure is Not Organization.' Building upon the account of 'organizational capability' that Waterman developed within this paper, Peters soon began to lobby for two further changes within the developing s-framework. He argued for the inclusion of 'skill' and for the removal of 'sequencing,' which it was suggested was a poor fit with the remaining 's' variables.

Keen to monetize their, still emergent research McKinsey and Co. quickly began to offer workshops on what was, at that point a 'six-s' model. Pascale attended an early workshop and was soon invited to host subsequent iterations. Julian Phillips of McKinsey, who had also contributed to these workshops, soon added his voice to those suggesting that 'sequencing' should be dropped from the model in favour of 'staff.' Commenting upon this mooted development, Pascale and Athos ([1981] 1986: x) observe that none of those who had worked to develop the emerging and still, skeletal, model was truly comfortable with 'sequencing.' Consequently this factor was dropped from the emerging framework by common consent. 'And since Peters was proposing that "people" and "power" needed somehow to be included (Athos was by then adding "aggregates of people" [to the teaching materials that he had developed to use] at Harvard), it was also possible to agree that Staff was an addition which resolved various concerns.'

Thus, the now familiar McKinsey 7-S framework came to be:

- Strategy
- Structure
- Systems
- Staff
- Style
- Skills
- Superordinate Goals (Shared Values)

Crainer (1997) offers an account of the development of the *McKinsey* 7-S framework that is similar to that offered by Pascale and Athos. Yet, he adds a competitive dynamic that is under-played within 'ready-made' accounts of the excellence project. Thus, Crainer suggests that the excellence project developed as Tom Peters' employers the consulting firm, McKinsey and Co. sought to defend the company's market position and reputation against two key competitors: namely, the Boston Consulting Group and Bain and Co. It is worth noting, however, that Crainer's account of the genesis of the excellence project, in common with that recently rendered by Peters (2018), focuses primarily on the activities of the Boston Consulting Group (BCG).

Both Crainer and Peters remind us that in the early 1970s the Boston Consulting Group had developed and, successfully, marketed two management tools, 'The Experience Curve' (which suggested that those companies which have accumulated significant experience in the production of particular goods and services would reap the benefits of reduced unit costs) and the 'Boston Matrix' (which offered the managers of conglomerate organizations a tool that, it was claimed, would measure market growth potential across its portfolio). Within McKinsey there were fears that market developments of this sort were raising the reputation and profile of competitors at the expense of 'the firm.' In an attempt to reverse this process, the senior management of McKinsey cast around for something that might serve to rebuild their reputation in the marketplace as truly leading-edge strategic thinkers (see McDonald [2013] 2020). In 1977[1] following a period of reflection, McKinsey launched three new practices configured around 'Strategy,' 'Organization' and 'Operations.' Together, these 'practices' were instructed to consider the relationship between strategy, structure and effectiveness.

Tom Peters, as we intimated earlier, was duly recruited to the 'Organization Practice' and was soon dispatched on an eight-week trip to gather knowledge and information on the practices of 'effective organizations.' This trip, Peters and Waterman (1982: 4) tell us, involved extensive discussions with key business executives and, later, visits to 'a dozen business schools in the United States and Europe' (5). Building on these discussions and upon a review of the published literature on 'effectiveness,' the 'Organization Practice' began to argue that focusing upon 'strategy' and 'structure' was unproductive in the absence of a more detailed appreciation of organizational processes. Defining the problem in such negative terms was, of course, relatively easy for the 'Organization Practice.' Stating a positive solution to the problem identified, however, proved to be more problematic both for clients and for colleagues. Indeed Crainer (1997) notes that early reaction to the stirrings of Peters and his collaborators was muted within *McKinsey* and among its clientele. Elaborating upon this point, Crainer (1997) observes that between 1978 and 1979 Peters and his colleagues pitched their reflections on 'organizational effectiveness' to a range of major organizations, including *DART, Royal Dutch Shell, PepsiCo* and *Siemens* but were unable to secure any clients for the effectiveness practice.[2] These organizations (and others like them) were, it seems, amenable to the broad thrust of the argument but doubted that this might be codified and applied to produce tangible business outcomes. *Business Horizons*, however, was sufficiently intrigued to invite Waterman, Peters and Phillips to publish an account of the project and its core concerns (Waterman, Peters and Phillips, 1980). This article was, we suggest, truly instrumental to the successful launch of the excellence project for in the 18 months following its publication, Peters responded to invitations which saw him give 200 speeches and 50 workshops on 'excellence.' Within McKinsey and Co., however, not all were supportive (see Collins, 2022). Indeed Peters (2018) offers crucial insights on the machinations within McKinsey and Co., which shaped his experience in this period, and later, his removal from the firm. Thus, Peters' (2018) account of the genesis of the excellence project, while offering a broad endorsement of the origin narratives developed by Crainer (1997) and by Pascale and Athos [1981] (1986), adds a new dimension to this discussion. Crucially this narrative invites us to confront the on-going political machinations within 'the firm' which, as Peters sees it, hampered the development of the excellence project. This more political rendering of the origin narrative gives a starring to Ron Daniel, then, the Managing Director of the firm.

Ron Daniel, Peters (2018: 60) tells us, 'had noticed . . . that McKinsey provided sound advice to its clients, but far too often the grand plans failed the implementation test.' To remedy this, Peters tells us that the Managing Director of the firm chose to launch 'mostly beneath the radar' (60) an 'organizational effectiveness' practice in parallel to the 'strategy' and 'operations' practices that had, in contrast, been introduced to the public with some fanfare. Recognizing that Tom Peters had recently completed a PhD, focused upon 'implementation,' Ron Daniel secured his appointment to the organizational effectiveness practice. Soon afterwards, Peters (2018: 60) was dispatched 'on an unlimited travel budget . . . in pursuit of the best and most progressive and provocative thinking.' These progressives and provocateurs (located within corporations and within academic institutions), Peters (2018: 61 ellipses in original) tells us led him to the conclusion 'that what makes an organization soar was . . . "the soft stuff" . . . the nonlinear "people stuff." Yet he complains that the presentations around these themes that were offered 'to McKinsey grandees were met mostly with indifference' (61) if not outright hostility. In an attempt to manage this emerging, but deeply problematic situation Peters (2018: 61) reports that he embarked upon an insurgency designed to enrol like-minded 'renegades' who understood instinctively 'what McKinsey-ites considered secondary – the messy "implementation bit" was indeed the difference between winning and losing.' This insurgency, however, did not go un-noticed:

> As I gained traction, McKinsey traditionalists fought back. Through my network, I managed to get an op-ed published in *The Wall Street Journal* that was all about the impact of corporate culture on business results and implicitly (pretty explicitly, to be honest) downgraded the role of strategy. I was told that the head of the New York Office actually went to Daniel in an effort to get me fired. But Daniel remained steadfast; in fact such controversy and publicity around "McKinsey ideas" was just what he had been looking for.
>
> (Peters, 2018: 61)

Peters (2018: 61) credits Herb Henzler, a 'renegade' located within the German office as the source of the resources necessary to sustain the nascent excellence project. It was Henzler, he suggests, who persuaded *Siemens* to fund another round-the-world, fact-finding trip for the Organization Practice. This trip was, however, quite unlike that previously undertaken. While the first phase of research conducted by Peters had been content to quiz academics and leading executives, this second trip was designed to review practices within 'the world's top companies.'

In a few moments we will consider the manner in which Peters and Waterman came to codify these stirrings on business excellence. Yet, before we turn to this issue, it will be useful to shift focus once more.

So far we have considered the competitive context of the consulting industry in the 1970s. Furthermore, we have acknowledged the internal, political machinations that shaped conduct within McKinsey and Co. during this period. Yet, we have largely neglected the broader context of business excellence and the forces (re)shaping American business and, beyond this, US politics in the late 1970s. It is now time to address these issues.

The Broader Context of Excellence

In our account of the development of the McKinsey 7-S Framework, we offered reflections on the politics of the consulting industry and an account of the internal machinations of McKinsey and Co. Following Latour (1987) these reflections have been designed to secure an account of the developing architecture of business excellence at that point in time when its core ideas and practices remained highly conditional and more than a little controversial. In this section, while accepting that it is important to understand the context of the consulting industry and the internal problems of McKinsey we will shift focus to acknowledge the peculiarities of the socio-economic context that characterized America – and much of Western Europe – during the 1970s and early 1980s.

And why must we pause to consider this? The answer, as we shall see, is reasonably straightforward: it is this context and the sense of crisis which it precipitated that made Peters' stirrings on effectiveness substantial, his representations on business excellence real and his manifesto for change appealing to a mass-market audience (see Saunders and Wong, 1985; Kauffman, 1993; Byrne, 2001; Bogner, 2002).

The Recession of the Early 1980s

From 1981 to 1983, America endured a deep business recession that was, in an apparent reversal of the logic of Keynesian economics, marked by rising prices. Hyatt (1999) captures the situation rather well. At this time, he notes, America had an unemployment rate in excess of 10%, an inflation rate approaching 15% and a banking interest rate in excess of 20%. This set of economic circumstances, the worst America had suffered in five decades, led to street scenes which many believed had been consigned to an earlier period of history. *The Observer* (quoted in Baskerville and Willett, 1985), for example, reported that in Washington, DC 17,000 people had queued for five hours to receive food handouts. Placing this queue in a broader setting, it may be useful to observe that the *American Bureau of Census Statistics* reported that in the year following the publication of *In Search of Excellence*, 34.4 million Americans (some 12% of the population) were living below what was agreed to be the poverty line.

Americans in our experience are open, welcoming and kind. Yet, perhaps uniquely they subscribe to a particular belief as to the virtues and the relative standing of their homeland. In short, many Americans seem to believe and will loudly assert that theirs is 'the best country in the world.' For a variety of reasons – not least of which would be the absence of agreed, reliable metrics – we decline to debate the virtues of such claims. We will, however, pause to observe that by the early 1980s, it was becoming increasingly difficult to voice this belief publicly. Indeed there was for many Americans at this time, the feeling that things were going badly wrong in their country. This feeling – especially troublesome for a population encouraged to think of itself as top-dog – was reinforced by the impression that while America and Americans were suffering, others, (in popular imagination 'the Japanese') had experienced an 'economic miracle' and were, as our American relatives would suggest, 'making out like bandits.'

The Japanese Miracle

Fears regarding Japan's economic success and the growing dominance of the Asian economies more generally had, of course, been troubling a number of key commentators and many ordinary Americans before the recession of 1981–1983. As early as 1970, Kahn (1970) had published *The Emerging Japanese Superstate*, which argued that Japanese per capita income would exceed that of the US by the year 2000. By 1978, however, Kahn (Kahn and Pepper, 1978) had revised his forecast and was now suggesting that the Japanese mission – to catch up with the West – would be accomplished by 1980. Commenting on the shifting balance of trade between the US and Japan, Saunders and Wong (1985) point out that in 1970 America had a $1 billion trade deficit with Japan. Yet, they report that by 1984 the US-Japanese trade gap had grown to $33 billion. Little wonder, perhaps, that Khan's futurology (mocked by more than two decades of economic stagnation within Japan) was both alarming and persuasive by the early 1980s.

Concerns over the apparently inexorable rise of the Japanese economy soon led a great number of industrialists, politicians and policy-makers to ponder a) the root causes of Japan's economic miracle and b) the factors undermining America's faltering economy. Perhaps the most lucid statement on the power and potential of the Japanese economy was prepared by Pascale and Athos ([1981] 1986). Reflecting upon the prospects for the reform of American management, Pascale and Athos offered a stark commentary on the rise and rise of Japan:

> In 1980 Japan's GNP was third highest in the world and if we extrapolate current trends, it would be number one by the year 2000. A country the size of Montana, Japan has virtually no physical resources, yet it supports over 115 million people (half the population of the United States), exports $75 billion worth more goods than it imports, and has an investment rate as well as a GNP growth rate which is twice that of the United States. Japan has come to dominate in one selected industry after another – eclipsing the British in motorcycles, surpassing the

Germans and Americans in automobile production, wresting leadership
from the Germans and Americans and overcoming the United States'
historical dominance in businesses as diverse as steel, shipbuilding,
pianos, zippers and electronics . . . Japan is doing more than a little
right. And our hypothesis is that a big part of that "something" has only
a little to do with such techniques as its quality circles and lifetime
employment . . . we will argue that a major reason for the superiority of
the Japanese economy is their managerial skill.

(Pascale and Athos, [1981] 1986: 20–21)

Elaborating on the fundamental skill of Japanese management (and the reason for Japan's growth and continuing success), Pascale and Athos offered a
cultural analysis. They suggested that US managers had played a zero-sum
game confronting employee collectives in order to secure compliance with
managerial orders, whereas Japanese managers had toiled to develop collaborative relationships with 'enterprise unions,' and in so doing had manufactured organizational cultures aligned to the pursuit of innovation and
customer satisfaction (see Fukuda, 1988).

The early chapters of the analysis developed by Pascale and Athos
[1981] (1986), were built squarely upon the suggestion that US business
could learn much from the practice of management in Japan. Nonetheless,
the authors were keen to remind their readers that there remained within
the US economy sufficient pockets of good practice to sustain the hope
that the American economy might manage its own way out of the crisis.
Yet, as their argument proceeds the tone of the analysis offered by Pascale
and Athos changes and hardens. Indeed by the time *The Art of Japanese
Management* concludes, Pascale and Athos seem to have settled on the
understanding that management in the US was, by the late 1970s, macho,
short-termist, ill-suited to the present crisis, and so, singularly incapable of meaningful reform (see Collins, 2022). By 1981, therefore, there
seemed to be two routes available to America. Americans could work *like*
the Japanese or – given the significant increase in overseas direct investment flowing from Tokyo – they could work *for* the Japanese. Peters and
Waterman (1982), however, rejected this line of analysis. They offered
In Search of Excellence to the reader as an attempt to (re)educate American managers in the distinctive capabilities of *American* management. In
this regard, *In Search of Excellence* is based upon a simple, yet plausible
conceit that has come to underpin much of 'popular management' (see
Collins, 2001; Collins and Porras, [1994] 2004; Covey, [1989] 2020).
Thus Peters and Waterman argued that the successful US organizations,
which constitute their analytical frame a) exhibited core common practices, which in being b) portable within and between the various sectors of

the US economy offered c) a distinctively American manifesto for change and renewal. Utilizing McKinsey's 'happy atom,' Peters and Waterman (1982), therefore, echoed elements of the analysis developed by Pascale and Athos [1981] (1986), while rejecting its final conclusions. Both partnerships agreed that America's economic decline was to be regarded as a product of imbalances in the approach to management that had emerged in the US during the 1950s and 1960s. American managers, they warned, had become fixated upon the 'hard-s' factors of business *strategy, structure* and *systems* and had lost sight of the importance of *staff, style, skill* and *superordinate* goals: the 'soft-s' factors required to breathe life into strategies, structures and systems. Yet, at this point the narrative developed by Peters and Waterman departs from that outlined by Pascale and Athos. Where Pascale and Athos suggested that US business was pretty much,incapable of purposeful change and reform, Peters and Waterman simply insisted that American leaders could return balance (and hence success) to the US economy through a programme of cultural change and realignment.

In an attempt to demonstrate the presence of US organizations which had successfully balanced the 'soft-s factors' of business, and in so doing, had out-performed those who focused only upon a narrower range of 'hard' concerns, Peters and Waterman (1982) built their analysis of business excellence upon the research that had been commissioned by *McKinsey*. This commission had obliged Peters, Bennett and others to:

- analyse publicly available date on performance,
- review the literature on organizational performance published during the previous 25 years,
- engage in structured interviews with personnel drawn from those organizations that had performed at a consistently high level during this period.

Discussing the development of their research programme, Peters and Waterman tell us that they initially identified a group of 75 companies whose rating on six measures of financial performance made them leaders in their respective fields. These indicators being:

- compound asset growth,
- compound equity growth,
- average ratio of market to book value,
- average return on total capital,
- average return on equity,
- average return on sales.

We should note that this first frame of 75 companies chose to exclude banks and financial institutions because it was suggested that the regulatory environment shaping conduct within this context was sufficiently distinctive to skew results. Commenting upon this exclusion, Peters and Waterman, however, hinted that they would defer the consideration of excellence within banking and finance to a later study.

From the initial grouping of seventy-five firms, Peters and Waterman tell us that they subsequently rejected 13 companies as failing to reflect the pattern of American business. It is worth noting, however, that *Schlumberger*, a European high technology company, somehow slipped through this screen and was retained within the excellent panel of companies (see Saunders and Wong, 1985).

Having removed 13 cases from the initial sample, Peters and Waterman tell us that they then chose to analyse the remaining 62 cases in the light of the six financial performance indicators noted above. To qualify as 'excellent' the authors decided that each company would have to post financial results in at least four of the six selected measures, which placed it in the top half of its industry. On the basis of this analysis of performance, Peters and Waterman decided that eighteen of the remaining 62 companies were (probably) excellent but did not quite meet all of their criteria. A further 30 companies, however, were agreed to be excellent according to the criteria outlined above, while a final grouping of fourteen companies (the focus of Chapter three) were said to represent exemplars of excellence. This stratified sample was refined by 'boosting' the scores awarded for innovation. Yet, the processes underpinning this approach remain opaque. Indeed, the circumstances under which 'innovation' constituted in terms of organizational 'responsiveness' might be made the subject of an agreed and reliable process of 'boosting' is left solely to the imagination of the reader!

Table 2.1 identifies the long list of 62 excellent companies selected for praise by Peters and Waterman. Table 2.2 meanwhile lists the 43 companies taken to be (somehow) properly representative of American business. They were selected for analysis within *In Search of Excellence*. Table 2.3 acknowledges the 14 'exemplars of excellence' that we will consider in-depth within chapter three.

Peters and Waterman (1982) insist that the excellent companies listed in Tables 2.2 and 2.3, despite their quite different industrial and commercial settings, are culturally similar. Elaborating upon this point the authors argued that their excellent organizations displayed and were defined by eight common attributes.

The 'eight attributes of excellence' are, of course, now central to the excellence project, and so, feature prominently in student textbooks and in the on-line crib guides that we highlighted in our introductory remarks. But the so-called attributes of excellence did not always occupy this central position.

Table 2.1 The long-list of 62 Excellent Companies highlighted by Peters and Waterman (1982)

Allen-Bradley	Amdahl	American Airlines	Arco	Atari
Avon	Bechtel Boeing Fluor	Blue Bell	Bristol-Myers	Caterpillar Tractor
Cheeseborough-Pond's	Dana Corporation	Data General	Delta Airlines	Digital Equipment
Disney Productions	Dow Chemicals	Du Pont	Eastman Kodak	Emerson Electrical
Exxon	Frito-Lay	General Electric	General Foods	General Motors
Gould	Hewlett-Packard	Hughes Aircraft	IBM	Ingersoll-Rand
Intel	Johnson & Johnson	K-Mart	Levi Strauss	Lockheed
Marriott	Mars	Maytag	McDermott	McDonald's
Merck	Minnesota Mining & Manufacturing	National Semiconductor	NCR	Polaroid
Procter & Gamble	Raychem	Revlon	Rockwell	Schlumberger
Standard Oil/ Amoco	Texas Instruments	Tupperware	Wal-Mart	Western Electric
Westinghouse	Xerox			

Table 2.2 The 43 Excellent Companies highlighted by Peters and Waterman (1982)

Allen-Bradley	Amdahl	Avon
Bechtel	Boeing	Bristol-Myers
Caterpillar Tractor	Cheeseborough-Pond's	Dana Corporation
Data General	Delta Airlines	Digital Equipment
Disney Productions	Dow Chemical	Du Pont
Emerson Electrical	Fluor	Frito-Lay (Pepsico)
Hewlett-Packard	Hughes Aircraft	IBM
Intel	Johnson & Johnson	K-Mart
Levi-Strauss	Marriott	Mars
Maytag	McDonald's	Merck
National Semiconductor	Procter & Gamble	Raychem
Revlon	Schlumberger	Standard Oil/ Amoco
Texas Instruments	Tupperware	Wal-Mart
Wang Laboratories		

Table 2.3 The 14 exemplars of excellence highlighted by
Peters and Waterman (1982)

The Exemplars of Excellence
Bechtel
Boeing
Caterpillar Tractor
Dana
Delta Airlines
Digital Equipment
Emerson Electric
Fluor
Hewlett-Packard
IBM
Johnson & Johnson
McDonald's
Procter and Gamble
3M

Indeed, it has been suggested that they were, in fact, a late addition to the project; a pragmatic adjustment that arose as Peters prepared a presentation to be delivered within the Munich office of McKinsey and Co. in 1979.

The Eight Attributes of Excellence

By 1979, having spent two years trying to come to terms with the nature of organizational effectiveness, Peters had developed a large slide-show presentation designed to introduce the excellence project to potential clients. Two-day presentations, illuminated by a deck of 700 slides, were offered to clients across the McKinsey estate. While preparing for a presentation within the Munich office, however, Peters was offered some crucial advice by colleagues. While the members of *Siemens* who had attended one of the two-day show-cases on excellence had warmed to the arguments offered by Peters, he was warned that *PepsiCo*, which had requested a similar audience, would demand greater thematic coherence. In an attempt to provide this coherence, Peters toiled to develop a more concrete 'take away' for his audience and duly developed an outline of business excellence around what would soon become, simply, 'the eight attributes of business excellence.'[3] The attributes outlined by Peters and Waterman (1982) are – of course – as follows:

(1) A Bias for Action

Excellent companies, Peters and Waterman (1982) argue, engage in traditional planning activities but address these in a fashion that understands
the challenge of implementation. Commenting upon the manner in which
their excellent organizations interact with the planning process, Peters and
Waterman argue that the also-rans of the business world are overly reliant
on traditional forms of planning. These conventions, the authors argue, dis-
courage risk-taking and responsiveness because they consider 'hard' data
as the only reliable basis for managerial action. Highlighting the business
dangers that arise in connection with what they term, *paralysis by analysis*
Peters and Waterman (1982) argue that their excellent organizations simply
refuse to accept that all decisions have to be backed by 'hard' data and/
or more conventional forms analysis. Instead of making excessive use of
committees, Peters and Waterman argue that excellent companies maintain
a bias for action, a willingness to try out new ideas and a willingness to
take risks.

(2) Close to the Customer

Excellent companies, Peters and Waterman argue, gear their innovation
and their strategies, structures and systems to meeting, and exceeding, the
expectations of the customer. Where a product or a system had failed to
satisfy customer needs, we are told the excellent organization would have a
simple means of identifying this and a channel to ensure that this information is fed back to the appropriate personnel within the organization, so that
the problem would be remedied. In this regard the excellent organizations
are said to be 'close to the customer' by instinct and by design.

(3) Autonomy and Entrepreneurship

Excellent companies value entrepreneurship. To encourage enterprise and to
encourage people to develop and to try out new ideas, Peters and Waterman
observe that excellent companies ensure that departments and units remain
small enough to allow for *ad hoc* exchanges and informal networking.

(4) Productivity Through People

While it is very easy to mouth the words that people are the organization's
key asset, Peters and Waterman insist that excellent companies pay more
than lip service to this idea. Thus, the excellent companies, we are assured,
work to ensure that people are recognized and rewarded for their contribution so that they, in fact, feel valued. And since the employees of the

excellent organizations truly feel valued, they are the authors tell us, encouraged to commit to the mission even when this proves taxing.

(5) Hands-On; Value-Driven

Leaders of excellent companies are just that. Indulging a separation that has become commonplace within popular management (see Bennis, 2009), Peters and Waterman tell us that the leaders of excellent organizations secure performance from others because they understand that their role extends beyond that of management. In an attempt to bring some clarity to this (largely implicit) conceptualization of leadership, Peters and Waterman insist that leaders are visible. They manage by walking about. They lead by example and in so doing maintain close contact with staff and with customers. Leaders, in short, work to foster key values which bind people together in the pursuit of common goals.

(6) Stick to the Knitting

Excellent companies, Peters and Waterman argue retain a laser-like focus upon the key competence of the organization. This attribute makes the excellent organizations rather unusual for it suggests that they had ignored the consultancy advice peddled throughout the 1970s which had led to the development of m-form and conglomerate organizational structures (Guest, 1992).

(7) Simple Form, Lean Staff

Organizations should be staffed by individuals who are skilful, innovative and committed. Few, we suggest, would choose to disagree with this statement. The challenge, of course, is to retain the services of such individuals while animating them to produce value for the customer. Peters and Waterman argue that the excellent organizations secure staff commitment and application because they have adopted an organizational design that enables this high level of performance. This design template the authors label, 'simple form, lean staff' to remind us that the excellent companies are successful precisely because they have deliberately adopted simple, team-based structures, designed to maximize interaction, and so, innovation.

(8) Loose-Tight Properties

This, the final of the eight attributes of excellence is, we suggest, usefully considered as an extension of the 'simple form, lean staff' commitment insofar as it, too, has been designed to show-case the manner in which the excellent companies confront and conquer a key paradox. To explain: excellent companies value innovation and risk-taking, and so, they hire and reward free-thinking people. To reap the rewards of innovation and to ensure that innovation remains customer-focused, some system of controls will, of course, be required. Yet, in seeking to channel and to control innovation, managers run the risk that they will actually stifle purposeful development. To overcome this paradox, excellent companies, we are told, reward loyalty and foster commitment by granting freedom and autonomy!

On its own terms *In Search of Excellence* – constituted in and through the *McKinsey* 7-S framework and the eight attributes of excellence – offers a plausible, perhaps even a seductive, manifesto for change. After all, who could disagree with the idea that successful companies should direct their efforts towards meeting customer needs?

Who could disagree with the idea that companies, which demand innovation from their staff must be prepared to reward those forms of conduct and interaction that beget invention?

And who, nowadays, would publicly disparage the idea that companies need to strike a balance between the social and the technical between the 'soft-s' and the 'hard-s' factors if they are to secure useful outcomes?

Yet, in spite of this commonsense appeal there are, as we shall see, key problems with the analysis offered by Peters and Waterman.

Key Criticisms of *In Search of Excellence*

Perhaps the most commonly voiced criticism raised against the excellence project appeared in *Business Week* in November 1984 (05/11/1984) as a cover-story entitled 'Who's excellent now?' Reviewing the track record of the companies, which Peters and Waterman (1982) had identified as 'excellent,' this headline article observed that, just two years after the publication of *In Search of Excellence*, one third of the 'excellent' firms were suffering some degree of financial distress. Three years later, writing for *The Financial Analysts Journal,* Clayman (1987) offered a similar account, which seemed to confirm that the excellent companies had begun to falter almost as soon as the ink was dry on *In Search of Excellence*.

We should not overlook the importance of the critiques developed by *Business Week* and by *The Financial Analysts Journal*. The *Business Week* article, for example, is important because it is so often repeated. Indeed for nearly four decades the authors of *In Search of Excellence* have been obliged to respond to its core claims. Many of those who have rehearsed and repeated the *Business Week* critique do so because they assume that it is fatal to the excellence project. Yet, despite its frequent repetition, this line of attack is actually rather limiting as the basis for a critical review of *In Search of Excellence*. Three points of clarification are worthwhile.

Firstly, we should note that the criticisms offered by *Business Week* and by *The Financial Analysts Journal*, while perhaps accurate over the short-term, are highly sensitive to the time-period under scrutiny and are, in fact, challenged by later work which confirms the economic success of the excellent organizations over a longer timeframe (see Ackman, 2002). Secondly, it is worth noting that the *Business Week* attack tends to suggest that the excellent organizations faltered because of internal managerial failures, which Peters and Waterman (1982) had failed to consider. Yet, Woolfson and Foster (1988: 6–7) remind us that many US organizations suffered distress in the early 1980s. Looking at the case of *Caterpillar*, one of the 'exemplars' of excellence, they remind us that the 40% decline in overseas sales experienced by this company in 1982 is largely explained by changes in the relative value of the dollar. Thus, Woolfson and Foster argue that *Caterpillar* (in common with a host of the excellent organizations) lost market share in this period because a significant rise in the value of the dollar simply made US exports prohibitively expensive. Thirdly, we should acknowledge that while the critiques voiced by *Business Week* and by Clayman (1987) appear to attack the very foundations of the excellence project they actually accept much of its constitution. Thus, the *Business Week* critique seems to accept a) that there exists a separate and distinctive category of excellent firms who b) stand proud of their peers because of c) their distinctive managerial practices, but it mocks Peters and Waterman for being, as Stewart ([2009] 2010: 246) has claimed 'particularly bad stock pickers.' Fortunately, other commentators have looked longer and harder at the work of Peters and Waterman and, from an informed position, have generated critical reviews of the excellence project, which usefully question its outputs *and* the ideas, orientations and suppositions that constitute its inputs. One of the earliest of these, more critical, reviews was produced by Carroll (1983) just as the excellence phenomenon began to secure traction in the US.

A Disappointing Search

Carroll's (1983) critique of *In Search of Excellence* is significant, beyond being perhaps the first genuinely critical voice raised in opposition to the excellence project, because it demands that we locate the excellence project within a larger social-political context. David Guest (1992) offers a similar line of criticism. Indeed taking issue with a complaint voiced by Peters and Waterman (1982), Guest argues that *In Search of Excellence* is seductive but flawed. *In Search of Excellence* is he warns right enough to be dangerously wrong. In an attempt to substantiate their criticisms, Guest and Carroll, like others (see also Aupperle, Acar and Booth, 1986; Van der Merwe and Pitt, 2003), analyse the methodological and conceptual construction of the excellence project, and in so doing, highlight key failings, which the *Business Week* article had simply ignored.

The Methodological Critique

In Search of Excellence is, of course, based upon a small sample of US firms, which the authors claim have been successful over an extended period of time. Peters and Waterman authors argue that these successful firms have attributes in common that define them and which separate them from their less successful counterparts. Yet, there are problems with the sampling technique adopted by Peters and Waterman. For example, both Carroll and Guest observe that, in preparing their sample of firms, Peters and Waterman employed unorthodox and largely unscientific methods. They note, for example, that the sample of 'excellent' companies begins with an *ad hoc* grouping that reflects the orientations and predispositions of journalists and colleagues rather than, say, any more meaningful account of business fundamentals. Furthermore, they suggest that this initial and *ad hoc* sample becomes progressively corrupted and skewed as the authors allow their own biases and orientations to adjust the population in an *ad hoc*, self-serving and thoroughly unscientific manner.

In addition to the design problems noted above, Guest and Carroll observe that the methodology of the excellence project is poorly executed. Leaving aside the fact that financial measures of performance may not offer a true representation of business fundamentals and may be managed to reflect more local decisions relating to taxation and dividend payments, for example, both Guest and Carroll observe that a great deal of weight is placed on anecdote and idiosyncratic recollection. Indeed, they observe that the data collected on the organizational practices of their 'excellent' organizations is undeserving of this grandiose and pseudo-scientific label for it is, too often, the outcome of a simple chat with a senior executive who would have obvious incentives to portray the organization and his role (very few women appear in the book!) in a positive light. Finally on the issue of methodology, Carroll (1983) observes that Peters and Waterman fail to study a less-than-excellent population, in tandem with their supposed exemplars of excellence. This failure to constitute what amounts to a control group means that we cannot be sure that the attributes of excellence are, in fact, *peculiar to, and characteristic of, excellent firms*. In this sense the excellence hypothesis is 'non-falsifiable' insofar as the methodology is constitutionally incapable of uncovering information that would refute the idea that excellent firms a) have attributes in common and that it is b) these eight attributes which deliver business excellence (see also Rosenzweig, 2007).

Together with such methodological failings there are a range of related conceptual shortcomings.

The Conceptual Critique

In Search of Excellence makes what economists would term an 'heroic' assumption because it suggests that organizational success is a product of those magical things: managerial energy and commitment (see also Saunders and Wong, 1985). Countering this assumption, Carroll wonders why Peters and Waterman have been so dismissive of factors associated with the success of other notable companies and economies. Thus, Carroll (1983: 79) suggests that Peters and Waterman's account of excellence is flawed because it fails to recognize the ways in which factors such as 'proprietary technology, market dominance, control of critical raw materials, and national policy and culture' might have a bearing upon the fortunes of an organization:

> Unfortunately, the most perfect adherence to the eight lessons [of excellence] will probably not permit 20 years of success against an IBM unless there is some sort of protective technology. Similarly oil companies without access to lower-cost oil supplies will suffer regardless of how well they implement the lessons [of *In Search of Excellence*].
>
> (79).

Heller [1994] (1995:63) offers similar reflections on the excellence project, which suggests the presence of dissenting voices ignored by Peters and Waterman:

> Outside opinions of organisations are notoriously unreliable, but a few clear-eyed insiders knew that IBM was seriously deficient on perhaps half of the eight counts [deemed necessary for excellence].

Guest (1992) takes a slightly different tack on the attributes of excellence. He observes that Peters and Waterman seem to suggest that business excellence depends upon the presence of all eight organizational attributes.[4] Yet, since a number of the attributes identified by Peters and Waterman overlap, he asks whether it might be sufficient to hit a simple majority of the eight attributes and yet return excellent results.

Exploring this issue from an empirical perspective, Saunders and Wong (1985) suggest that the highly performing organizations that they studied showed, in fact, only a very limited commitment to the eight attributes of excellence outlined by Peters and Waterman (1982). Indeed, Saunders and Wong observe that while there is some evidence to suggest that successful organizations do commit to on-the-job training, have a preference for simple structures, and have adopted a management style that is tolerant of mistakes, there is, in truth, no evidence to suggest that business success derives from 'sticking to the knitting,' or from having a 'bias for action.' Indeed Saunders and Wong (1985) suggest that the more successful organizations in their study were, in fact, more planning orientated than their less-successful counterparts!

Van der Merwe and Pitt (2003) also question the extent to which firms would have to exhibit all eight of the attributes discussed by Peters and Waterman, and in so doing, rehearse three lines of critique. Firstly, they observe that, for Peters and Waterman, excellence is discussed in simple binary terms. Like pregnancy, it seems that you are either excellent or *not* excellent, there being no 'in-between' set of circumstances. Questioning this binary characterization, Van der Merwe and Pitt suggest that business excellence might more usefully be construed as a continuum of possibilities.

Reflecting further on the nature of this spectrum of possibilities, Van der Merwe and Pitt raise a second point of criticism. Noting that Peters and Waterman have produced a cultural appreciation of the business of management, which hinges around leadership, they question the efficacy of the authors' preferred cultural management strategies. Thus, Van der Merwe and Pitt argue that Peters and Waterman portray excellent organizations as culturally unified collectives. Yet, they counter that this simple-minded celebration of consensus prevents us from acknowledging conflict within the collective, and in so doing, effectively precludes the meaningful analysis of organizational politics. On the strength of this more political reading of management and organization, Van der Merwe and Pitt raise a third point of criticism, which invites us to consider the wider costs and benefits of the excellence project. Indeed, they suggest that the excellence project might well visit costs – technically known as 'externalities' – on other groups and constituencies who have simply been excluded from the analytical frame.

We could, of course, continue in this vein for quite some time. But there is no need to labour the point unduly: the excellence project is, it is now accepted, ill-conceived and poorly executed. It lacks context and the objectivity of view that historical reflection and *proper* research provide. There is little wonder, perhaps, that in some quarters *In Search of Excellence* is dismissed as an affront to the professionalism of management (see Hilmer and Donaldson, 1996). And yet, the core message of *In Search of Excellence* not only persists, it prevails!

Who now would question the assertion that management is at root a cultural endeavour, hinged upon the arts of persuasion?

Who within the ranks of senior management would now reject the idea that to commit to the organized life is to commit to on-going change and renewal?

And who now – beyond the realms of the academy (du Gay, 2000; Vine, 2020) – is an advocate for 'bureaucracy'?

The answer (almost) unnecessary to our rhetorical questions is, of course, no one because in concert with a few others Peters and Waterman (1982) have established and sustained a managerial manifesto that has provided a new way to think about; to talk about; and to practice the art of management. The problem being that so many critical commentaries on the excellence project simply fail to appreciate this general truth.

Why does this situation prevail? The answer of course is complex but at least part of a meaningful response to this question, we suggest, rests with an understanding that to countenance the failure of the conventional, academic critique would be a) to announce the triumph of faith over science whilst b) inviting deeper, critical reflection upon the nature of management and on the lived experience of social organization that few (managerialist) commentators have been willing to embrace.

Stewart ([2009] 2010: 245) flirts with this deeper, critical reflection but in the end chooses to rehearse the conventional line of critique. Thus, Stewart protests that the analysis developed by Peters and Waterman breaches normal academic conventions. *In Search of Excellence* is, he protests, flawed conceptually and methodologically. Furthermore, he warns us that the text is marshalled in a fashion that is not actually representative of the data-set. Thus Stewart [2009] (2010: 244) reminds us that while *In Search of Excellence* depends upon a panel of some 43 companies only 7 of these are discussed in-depth. Indeed he adds that the authors ignore fully 15 companies from their sample and pay, but, cursory attention to the remaining 20 'or so.'[5] Stewart, however, does seem to grasp, if only fleetingly, the limitations of this conventional critique. While lambasting Peters and Waterman as failed empiricists, for example, Stewart [2009] (2010: 268) pauses to venture the opinion that Peters is, in truth, 'a crypto-evangelist' who trades in hope and fear; preaching fantasies of change and redemption (while securing the acquisition of earthly riches that would humble the fantasies of lottery players). Yet, Stewart seems unwilling to pursue the threads of his developing realization. Consequently, he concludes by offering an analysis rooted in debunking (Collins, 2001), which is to say that he sneers at the gurus while disparaging those who would listen to them. Thus, Stewart ([2009] 2010: 316) avers that most gurus 'are best left to the trash can of history.'

Others however *have* been able to sustain a vision of Peters and Waterman that can facilitate a qualitatively different appreciation of the ways and means of *In Search of Excellence*. Maidique (1983), was, perhaps, among the first to grasp the broader appeal *In Search of Excellence*, although choosing to highlight its conceptual oversights and methodological failings. *In Search of Excellence* is, she warns, a hugely popular, if deeply flawed, text whose allure depends upon a revivalist tone. Highlighting the charm of this revivalist message, Maidique observes that *In Search of Excellence* builds and depends upon the positive nature of its core message. The text has, she tells us, a conversational style which is enlivened by the presence of colourful, evangelical prose (see also Mitchell, 1985; Saunders and Wong, 1985; Hyatt, 1999).

Huczynski's (1993) overview of the essence of 'guru theory' also invites us to consider the manner in which Peters, the failed scientist, attracts and secures converts to his cause. Importantly, however, Huczynski offers sustained analytical reflections on that which Maidique is inclined, simply, to state. Thus Huczynski argues that the gurus have successfully colonized our understanding of the world and its problems because they present a world of opportunities (and threats) built around an ideological focus which enhances the rights and privileges of management. Tracing the genealogy of 'guru theory,' Huczynski suggests that the pronouncements of modern gurus such as Peters and Waterman have clear continuities with earlier works prepared by the likes of Watson [1963] (2003) and Barnard (1968) and in many ways echo their suggestion that the primary function of the executive is to craft a moral code for others. Documenting the precise articulation of this moral code and compass, Huczynski suggest that guru theorizing tends to exhibit three, common, core traits and, within these traits 12 interdependent, complementary and overlapping features. Guru theory, therefore, articulates an understanding of the world of work which is:

1   readily communicable through acronyms, alliteration or slogans,
2   focused upon the presumed capacity which leaders have to change the conduct of others,
3   happy to assert that human thoughts and feelings are similarly malleable in the hands of the skilled leaders lauded at point two.

Exploring the second trait said to typify guru theorizing, Huczynski suggests that successful representations of managerial work have been designed to enhance the status of the intended purchaser. Marketable representations of managerial work he suggests:

4   Provide legitimation and self-affirmation for those engaged in managerial work. In other words, guru theory indulges the presumption that managers are truly special and genuinely heroic.
5   Build upon a unitary account of managerial work which suggests that there is no room for meaningful dissent with respect to organizational ends or indeed the means used to secure these goals.
6   Allow modifications which enable managers a) to tailor the model to local problems and contingencies and in so doing allow practitioners b)

to voice the suggestion that they have usefully and meaningfully acted on their own initiative.

7 Focus upon 'leadership' and in so doing suggest that colleagues will volunteer their support even to the point of altruism.

Examining the third trait, Huczynski focuses, unsurprisingly, on practical application. Thus, he argues that successful forms of guru theory:

8 promise control over market conditions otherwise notable for their volatility,

9 outline a limited number of steps that, in execution, will deliver useful, planned, change (see Collins, 1998 for an account of *n*-step guides),

10 suggest that the idea, tool or initiative enjoys universal applicability,

11 carry authorization or proof but not in the traditional academic or empirical sense. Commenting upon this Lischinsky (2008) observes that popular management ideas rarely build upon original empirical research but depend instead upon 'persuasive examples,'

12 has ready applicability and can be utilized without special tools or knowledge.

Pattison's (1997) analysis complements that offered by Huczynski (1993). Indeed it invites further reflection on what it might mean to be a 'management guru.'

Pattison acknowledges that the term, 'management guru' is now commonly used to label those who have made high-profile contributions to the field of popular management. Yet, he concedes that not all are inclined to accept that a term, which suggests spiritual enlightenment (see for example Jackson and Carter, 1998; Collins, 2021) should be applied to a sphere of life, that is, not simply strictly secular in its orientations but utterly Godless. Addressing this concern, Pattison draws on the work of Geertz (1993: 90), and in so doing, makes it plain that religious metaphor and allusion remain performative even in the absence of a visible deity.

Geertz (1993) suggests that religion is a) a system of symbols which acts b) to establish powerful, pervasive and long-lasting moods by c) formulating conceptions of a general order to human existence and by d) portraying these within a reality which e) makes particular patterns of thought and action necessary. Building upon this formulation, Pattison (1997: 39) suggests that management is 'a substantially, if mostly implicitly religious activity' and demonstrates this by sketching (36–37) an ideal management religion. Deconstructing the articles of faith that lie at the heart of management, he tells us that management has become if not quite a religion in the terms preferred by Geertz (1993) then certainly something steeped in religiosity. Thus, he argues that popular management theory is built upon the commitment of employees – the laity of the church of management if you will – even to the point of altrusim *and* the explicit rejection of past teachings. This dual commitment he tells us leads to a strong sense of corporate identity, which enables the formation of insider and outsider groupings. Those on the outside, he reminds us, are deemed to be lacking and hence marked as failures. Meanwhile, those who enjoy insider status are obliged to focus upon perfection and perfectability in order to maintain their privileged status and are assisted in this by charismatic leaders who demand, from their followers, some combination of individual responsibility and asceticism. Turning his attention to Tom Peters, Pattison pursues this focus upon self-control and the self-denial, necessary for the realization of the organizational mission. Thus Pattison (1997: 135) points out that while *In Search of Excellence* calls out and rejects earlier teachings (embodied in the persons of Robert McNamara and Peter Drucker), it simultaneously connects with the imagery of *The Old Testament* in insofar as it honours 'the faithful remnant' who like the Israelites in Egypt remained true to their calling, and so, rejected the false prophets who had deviated from the one, true path . . . of excellence.

Watson's (2001) account of the legacy of the excellence project is similarly interesting albeit less concerned with religious allusion. In common with Huczynski, Watson acknowledges the academic limitations of *In Search of Excellence*. Yet, Watson concedes that, despite its manifest failings, *In Search of Excellence* remains a substantial and persuasive text. Reflecting upon those characteristics that bring substance to a text otherwise separated from the architecture that sustains academic truth-claims, Watson protests that *In Search of Excellence* is a significant work because it reminds us that management has a moral as well as a technical dimension, and in making this point, successfully portrays employees as sentient humans and seekers and creators of meaning. Elaborating on this meaning-making, Watson suggests that *In Search of Excellence* is an important work for it advances and has popularized a basic and inescapable truth of management: that the meaning of management is, at root, the management of meaning.

Yet, Mitchell (1985) sounds a note of caution. Reviewing *In Search of Excellence* he concedes that this text is indeed significant for it reminds us that managing is a human endeavour.[6] However, he protests that Peters' and Waterman's concern with culture and with corporate symbolism is a triumph of form over substance. Indeed, he argues that *In Search of Excellence* has a concern with meaning, designed to obfuscate the realities of working, and a focus upon identity that is strictly manipulative.

In our next chapter, we will look again at these charges of obfuscation and manipulation as we consider business excellence in practice. Recognizing that criticisms of business excellence *in theory* are substantially correct yet largely irrelevant, we will offer a new and distinctive reappraisal of business excellence *in practice*. Indeed, we will demonstrate that there is much within the excellence project that has remained unspoken precisely because the conduct of its exemplars has often been *truly unspeakable*.

Concluding Comments

This chapter has offered critical reflections on the theory of business excellence and on the essential constitution of *In Search of Excellence*. Thus, we have offered an analysis of the genesis of the excellence project designed to explore the context(s), which made *In Search of Excellence* a reasonable if controversial response to the internal problems of McKinsey and Co. In addition we have examined the broader socio-economic concerns which shaped the US economy and polity in the late 1970s, and in so doing, made the core message of *In Search of Excellence* persuasive for a mass audience.

In common with many others, we have argued that *In Search of Excellence* is a flawed piece of research that is undermined by significant methodological and conceptual problems. Yet, while acknowledging the flawed science of the excellence project, we have insisted that *In Search of Excellence* remains largely immune to conventional forms of academic critique. Indeed we have argued that *In Search of Excellence* persists and prevails in the face of an academic onslaught sustained throughout the 1980s. Recognizing this resilience we have essayed a different, yet still critical, approach designed to acknowledge the manner in which the excellence project directs and controls its audience. Highlighting the essential religiosity of the excellence project we have rejected debunking. Instead we have argued that *In Search of Excellence* is a significant work, which remains worthy of scrutiny because it connects with us, not intellectually but viscerally, threatening our sense of self while promising relief and redemption. Yet, having advanced this understanding we have concluded with the suggestion that *In Search of Excellence* is, at root, a form of manipulation that builds and depends upon an obfuscation of the realities of working and managing. In our next chapter, we will pursue this understanding. Chapter three, therefore, will consider the lived experience of business excellence, the practices of those organizations vaunted as 'exemplars of excellence.' This analysis, as we shall see, reveals some very uncomfortable truths about the excellence project.

Notes

1 Peters and Waterman (1982: 3) render this just a little differently. They suggest that in 1977 McKinsey launched 'two internal task forces' to investigate 'strategy' and 'effectiveness.'

2 Of course Peters and Waterman (1982) suggest that *Royal Dutch Shell* offered the team the encouragement necessary to continue with the project.

3 See www.businessballs.com/strategy-innovation/in-search-of-excellence-tom-peters/

4 It is perhaps worth noting that at times Peters and Waterman (1982: 16–17) do seem to concede that it may not be necessary to secure all eight attributes.

5 Basic arithmetic suggests that this reference to '20 or so' case examples resolves in fact, to there being 21 excellent organizations who received, just cursory attention from Peters and Waterman (1982).

6 This is a point which, we should note, has eluded many commentators. Sloan's [1964] (1996) *My Years with General Motors* is for example notable for the absence of living, breathing people while Geneen's (Geneen with Moscow, 1986) account of his management practice is, perhaps notable for the almost complete absence of humanity! We say almost because Geneen did institute a policy designed to assist those employees and dependants who had developed problems with alcohol (see Collins, 2022).

3   *In Search of Excellence in Practice*

Introduction

In chapter two we considered excellence *in theory*. We discussed the conceptual-empirical foundations of *In Search of Excellence*, and we offered reflections on the manner in which Peters and Waterman (1982) developed and refined the analytical framework erected to advance the excellence project. Going beyond the limitations of the conventional critiques however we have located *In Search of Excellence* within the broader context of its formation. Thus, we have examined the social-political processes within and beyond McKinsey and Co, which shaped the constitution and elaboration of *In Search of Excellence*.

Academic reviews of *In Search of Excellence* have, of course, suggested that the research undertaken by Peters and Waterman is deeply flawed, both, conceptually *and* methodologically. We have endorsed this criticism yet we have dealt with it in an unusual manner. We have argued that while such critiques of the excellence project are, for the most part, pertinent, accurate and, often, well-made they have, nonetheless, failed to dent the appeal of *In Search of Excellence*. Accounting for this paradoxical outcome we have suggested that *In Search of Excellence* persists as an idea and prevails, as a set of, still cumulating, practices (see Collins, 2022) because the excellence project exists *not* to catalogue the world of management but to secure a change in our understanding of the essential nature of this endeavour. Pursuing this more rhetorical appreciation of the excellence project we have argued that there is now a need to forge a connection with the excellence project that can a) appreciate its essence and yet b) challenge its preferred reality in a manner that c) connects meaningfully with the lives and experiences of those who are obliged to interact with its core ideas. In this chapter, we offer this critique and connection. Challenging the excellence project at its strongest point we will consider the practices of the 'exemplars' of excellence. Building upon a range of sources, current and contemporary, we will seek answers to two key questions:

DOI: 10.4324/9781003341086-3

- What did Peters and Waterman actually know about the practices of those organizations which they vaunted as the very vanguard of business excellence in America?
- Do the recorded practices of these 'exemplary' organizations truly amount to an endorsement of the manifesto developed by Peters and Waterman (1982)?

Saunders and Wong (1985) begin to answer these questions. Offering an analysis of company performance that is based upon a sub-set of the excellent organizations, the authors observe that there is, in fact, little empirical evidence that high performing organizations demonstrate 'a bias for action.' Indeed Saunders and Wong observe that the successful organizations in their sample were, in fact, more planning oriented than their less successful counterparts. This is, of course, an interesting finding. It provides support, for example, to those who have suggested that business excellence is more usefully constituted as a spectrum of possibilities (see chapter two). Yet, while the work of Saunders and Wong is intriguing, it remains limited on two main counts. Firstly, this critique continues to accept the central *conceit* of the excellence project; namely, that there exists a group of exemplary organizations, alas still waiting to be named, whose success in business arises as a consequence of managerial leadership. Secondly, Saunders and Wong (1985) seem to accept that these 'excellent' practices are generalisable and, when more fully understood, may be usefully transported to other contexts.

In this chapter, we will essay a different approach. Mindful of the contribution of Saunders and Wong (1985), we will argue that what matters in the analysis of business excellence is not so much the *act* of planning as the *facts* of the plans developed. Reviewing the practices of those organizations celebrated as 'the exemplars of excellence' (see Table 3.1), we will demonstrate that the success enjoyed by these organizations is not due to the free interplay of the forces of competition, nor is it a result of their adherence to the attributes of excellence (see Table 3.2). The success is, in fact, more usefully acknowledged to reflect misconduct; *knavery* and on a large scale.

Documenting the (mis)conduct of those organizations hitherto celebrated as beacons for change and renewal, this chapter will reveal the realities of corporate practice that have been written-out of popular management *and* cast loose from mainstream management education. We offer this revelation so that we might write-in to the analysis of business excellence a new reality based upon an analysis of *actual* managerial practices. Thus, we will use our account of the realities of managerial practice to do what others have failed to achieve: we will re-think; re-view and re-write the business of excellence in order to reveal the manner in which its agenda for change is formed on foundations that deny the shabby, shameful interior of the corporate world.

Table 3.1 The 14 exemplars of excellence highlighted by
Peters and Waterman (1982)

The Exemplars of Excellence
Bechtel
Boeing
Caterpillar Tractor
Dana
Delta Airlines
Digital Equipment
Emerson Electric
Fluor
Hewlett-Packard
IBM
Johnson & Johnson
McDonald's
Procter and Gamble
3M

Table 3.2 The eight attributes of excellence according to Peters and Waterman (1982)

The Eight Attributes of Excellence
1 A Bias for Action
2 Close to the Customer
3 Autonomy and Entrepreneurship
4 Productivity through People
5 Hands-on; Value-Driven
6 Stick to the Knitting
7 Simple Form, Lean Staff
8 Simultaneous Loose-Tight Properties

Accordingly, this chapter is structured as follows: We will begin with reflections on the *real politic* of the corporate world (in the 1970s) before proceeding to offer a case report on each of the 14 'exemplars of excellence' highlighted by Peters and Waterman. These reports, as we shall see, respond to the key questions listed above and will demonstrate that what has been left unsaid about the business of excellence is often truly unspeakable!

The *Real Politic* of Business

The account of business excellence developed by Peters and Waterman (1982), as we have seen, amounts to a radical rejection of those forms management conduct, said to have been common in the immediate post-war period. *In Search of Excellence* tends to construct this attack in two ways. The first line of attack is largely structural in nature. This structural argument is based upon the suggestion that the 'hard' approach to management, common in the US throughout the 1950s and 1960s, had, by the 1970s, proved itself to be singularly incapable of addressing the competitive challenges posed by newly resurgent competitors such as Japan and South Korea. The second line of attack developed by Peters and Waterman is slightly different. It subsumes this structural argument within a narrative that personifies those said to be principally responsible for America's managerial malaise. Two key culprits are identified by Peters and Waterman (1982): they are Robert McNamara (formerly of *Ford*) and Peter Drucker.[1]

Pascale and Athos ([1981] 1986), co-creators of the 7-S framework, offer a similar analysis of America's problems. They begin their analysis by offering broad reflections upon 'Japanese' and 'American' systems of management. Yet, this structural-cultural account soon resolves to an emblematic comparison of two key individuals: Harold Geneen of the US conglomerate *ITT* and Konosuke Matsushita, the founder and head of the eponymous *Matsushita Corporation*. Pascale and Athos are, of course, publicly doubtful of Geneen's approach and legacy. They begin their analysis, however, with a key concession. They remind us that *ITT* had been transformed under Geneen's management. We should note that the company had reported 58 consecutive quarters of double digit growth under his leadership. Indeed sales had risen from $765.6 million in 1959 when Geneen joined the organization, to some $16.7 billion in 1977 (Geneen with Moscow, 1986: 1). Nonetheless, Pascale and Athos suggest that Geneen's time in office amounts to a failure. This failure is documented in two distinct ways. When Pascale and Athos are inclined to generosity, they offer a structural form of analysis. This structural rendering of the key issues suggests that *ITT* failed to develop the organizational systems and processes necessary to allow Geneen's successor to secure similar results. Yet, at other points in their text, Pascale and Athos are altogether less generous and are, in fact, inclined to personify the core problem. In this more personalized rendering of the issue, the authors suggest that Geneen failed *ITT* because he was, at root, a psychologically mal-adjusted bully who cared only for quarterly returns. Contrasting Geneen's conduct with that of Matsushita, Pascale and Athos complain that, while his Japanese counterpart had developed an open, long-term and collaborative culture, Geneen's approach was short-term in its orientation and, in being built upon coercive control, simply failed to secure useful, collaborative working relationships. This account of Geneen's approach amounts to a pretty devastating summary of his career and legacy. Yet in the light of other contemporary sources, there is reason to believe that the authors of *The Art of Japanese Management* may have been altogether too kind to their subject.

Reviewing the history of *ITT*, Sampson (1973) invites us to probe the reality of the corporate practices enabled by Geneen's apparent fixation on 'the numbers.' He notes that while *ITT* is notionally an American organization (and success story), it has been throughout its entire existence a foot-loose and determinedly self-serving corporation. Indeed Sampson challenges *ITT's* patriotic credentials. He reports, for example, that the company had continued to trade with Nazi Germany throughout World War II, funnelling business transactions with the Nazi regime through its South-American subsidiaries! Reflecting upon the Geneen era, Sampson draws our attention to the ways in which *ITT* had been willing to work with the CIA and with Nixon's Republican Party in order to further its corporate aims. Schoenberg (1985) has developed a similar account of *ITT* under Geneen. He begins, however, with a concession. He tells us that Geneen 'was ethically punctilious' (Schoenberg, 1985: 296). Yet, he quickly qualifies this assertion, and in so doing, reinforces the analysis developed by Sampson (1973). Geneen, Schoenberg (1985: 296–297) advises, 'was ethically punctilious, but according to his own quirky code. He would not let his people be blackmailed or shook down: but freely offered bribes were a regular part of ITT business practice.'

Looking in more detail at the pattern of bribery that developed within *ITT*, Schoenberg observes that America's Securities and Exchange Commission (SEC) had begun considering charges of overseas bribery against the company as early as 1968. It was only in March 1976, however, that *ITT* finally declared that it too had reason to believe that its employees had made (what the company coyly referred to as) unauthorized payments. In 1976, *ITT* made submissions to the SEC, which admitted that unauthorized payments of some $3.8 million had been made between 1971 and 1975. Schoenberg (1985: 311), however, makes it plain that this, frankly eye-watering concession of bribery proved to be a very significant under-estimation of *ITT's* wholesale misconduct:

> The final figure in the SEC's complaint was $8.7 million – to which ITT admitted. . . . The total figure included over $385,000 to Italian tax agents for a favourable settlement. . . . It also included $400,000 to Allende's opponents from 1970 through 1972, part of it channelled through a phony company called "Lone Star Shipping Corporation"

and charged off as PR expense. Although it is not clear, this was likely in addition to the $350,000 that went to Alessandri and his party before the popular election. The countries where the SEC has uncovered a pattern of bribery were Indonesia, Iran, the Philippines, Algeria, Nigeria, Mexico, Italy, Turkey and Chile.

Looking more closely at the Chilean case, Schoenberg reminds us that the election of Salvador Allende posed a serious problem for both *ITT* and the American State Department. Indeed, Schoenberg observes that fears concerning the nationalization of key assets held in Chile led the senior management of *ITT* to develop its own two-track strategy. This strategy involved the pursuit of a negotiated solution with the Allende administration as regards nationalization (and compensation) while simultaneously exploring an alternative path, which rejected simple bribery and corruption in favour of what we would now term, 'regime change.' Commenting upon *ITT's* willingness to support policies designed to unseat the democratically-elected Allende government, Schoenberg (1985: 297) tells us that Geneen was fully prepared to support a CIA-sponsored coup. He 'would have backed any plan to defeat Allende' and was, furthermore, fully willing to offer the CIA 'a million dollars of ITT's money' to render this solution.

Reviewing the exemplars of excellence within the context of this organized and deep-seated misconduct, we will argue that the corrupt(ing) practices underpinning Geneen's administration – shocking as these may be – are not, in fact, so unusual. Despite the wilful blindness of Peters and Waterman (1982) similar practices as we shall soon see, may be found within those organizations said to exemplify the very essence of business excellence. The remainder of this chapter will, therefore, offer 14 case reports on the exemplars of excellence, designed to alter our understanding of *In Search of Excellence* in theory and in practice. In what follows, therefore, we will swap the blind eye for a good one[2] so that we might reveal that which the excellence project (see Collins, 2022) has obscured; namely that the conduct of those organizations celebrated within *In Search of Excellence* was often venal and was, at times, downright criminal.

The Exemplars of Excellence

Bechtel

The *Bechtel Corporation* (as we now know it) was founded by Warren Bechtel in 1906 with the purchase of a single, but sizeable, piece of excavation equipment: a steam shovel, which had been developed for use on the construction of the Suez Canal. Despite the fact that the organization was not, then, incorporated, Warren Bechtel chose to play fast and loose with the legal technicalities then shaping business practice and ordered that the cab of his steam shovel should bear the legend 'W A BECHTEL CO' (McCartney, 1988: 22).

Thanks to a contract signed to deliver 106 miles of the Northwestern Pacific railway, Warren Bechtel was within a decade of the company's formation 'one of the most successful construction bosses' (McCartney, 1988: 22) in the United States and by the end of the 1920s had amassed a personal fortune of some $30 million.

Bechtel was born as a private company and unusually remains so until this day. Indeed Denton (2016: 7) reminds us that the company with revenues reported[3] to be in the region of $38 billion in 2013 remains, at root, very much a family firm. Documenting the growth and reach of this family business, Denton (2016: 7) observes that 'five generations of Bechtel men have harnessed and distributed much of the planet's natural resources – hydroelectricity, oil, coal, water, nuclear power, natural gas and now solar geothermal power and asteroids.' Offering a little more detail on Bechtel's projects and its contribution to the built environment, Denton (2016: 9–10) observes that this family firm has through a series of sub-contracting arrangements, constructed no fewer than:

- 95 airports,
- 17,000 miles of roads,
- 80 ports and harbours,
- 6,200 miles of railway,
- 100 tunnels including the Channel Tunnel that links England with France,
- 50 hydroelectric plants including the Boulder Dam,
- 30 bridges including the Oakland Bay-San Francisco Bridge,
- 30 military bases,
- 25 complete communities including Jubail, a £20 billion project undertaken on behalf of Saudi Arabia which is, perhaps, the single largest construction project in history.

In addition Bechtel has constructed nuclear power plants and nuclear waste treatment facilities. It has, furthermore, received contracts to clean up the devastation occasioned by the nuclear accidents at Three Mile Island and Chernobyl.

Peters and Waterman (1982) are staunch advocates for free market capitalism. Business excellence, the authors aver, is driven by competitive forces and depends *inter alia* upon getting close to the customer. Bechtel is similarly forceful in its advocacy of free market capitalism. Denton (2016) notes for example that the firm is publicly anti-government and anti-regulation. Yet, he warns that 'the Bechtel family owes its entire fortune to the US government'; to its contracts, connections and guarantees (Denton, 2016: 11).

Bechtel is plainly a very large and a very significant business entity. But is it, truly, excellent in the terms outlined by Peters and Waterman (1982)? Does its financial performance, for example, place it consistently towards the top half of its industry?

The simple answer to this question is that *we do not know*. A more candid answer however would be that *we simply cannot know* the answer to a question which surely lies at the very heart of the excellence project.

Commenting upon the manner in which the company operates, McCartney (1988: 135) observes that Bechtel is highly secretive and shares little meaningful information with the public. Indeed, reflecting upon the first ever annual report produced by *Bechtel, The Economist* (May 8th 1981) noted:

> An inquiry about profits to an otherwise charming Bechtel boss produces a sharp reminder to mind your manners. Such things remain the concern of the Bechtel family (who still own the vast majority of the stock) and a handful of top officers.

We should acknowledge of course that despite placing significant weight on published financial data Peters and Waterman (1982) did openly concede that a proportion of their panel of excellent companies had been unable (or unwilling) to provide the necessary financial information upon which their sampling process depended. Nonetheless, Peters and Waterman were adamant that the companies they labelled 'excellent' truly deserved this accolade. But what was the basis of such confidence?

Could a company which conducts its business through a complex assembly of sub-contracting arrangements truly be characterized as 'hands-on'?

Can Bechtel reasonably be characterized as being 'close to the customer'? Does the firm, for example, genuinely do whatever it takes to delight its clientele?

And was Bechtel then, and now, a value-driven organization?

McCartney (1988: 149–150) is publicly doubtful of Bechtel's customer orientation. Discussing the firm's work on behalf of the Libyan state, for example, McCartney notes that in 1969 Bechtel took steps to cover-up work that was not only sub-standard but unsafe. This Libyan cover-up was, we should note, no isolated incident! McCartney (1988: 153) observes that in 1974 Bechtel, while building a pipeline in Alaska, chose to falsify the certification of welding activity, and in so doing, subverted processes developed to assure the safety of its work. Furthermore, McCartney (1988: 158) alleges that throughout the 1970s, Bechtel participated in widespread corruption to secure its business. For example, he notes that Bechtel furnished senior Indonesian officials with bribes totalling some $3 million in order to secure contracts.

Probing the values underpinning its interactions with its customers, McCartney (1988) observes that the corporation's desire to secure contracts with the Egyptian state served to foster a deeply anti-Semitic corporate culture that has denied employment to those of the Jewish faith! We should note, however, that Bechtel's prejudice was not restricted to those born into Judaism. Bechtel was, in fact, similarly hostile to organized labour as evidenced by the mass termination of employees involved in a dispute at its Joppa production facility (McCartney, 1988: 168). Beyond this anti-unionism, it is worth noting that *Bechtel* also chose to engage in organizational practices that were openly prejudicial to its female employees and to its black employees – even as Peters and Waterman were exploring the seeds of business excellence. Denton (2016: 9–10), for example, notes that by 1975, Bechtel, the secretive organization that took care to maintain a low profile,

> was battling numerous lawsuits on grounds of sexism and racism. A sex discrimination case brought by 6,400 female employees claimed that Bechtel functions "like a [gentile[4]]men's club" that kept women employees – 4,000 of whom were college graduates – in low-paying secretarial jobs. Meanwhile, 400 black employees who claimed that they were victims of racial discrimination and harassment had filed a separate lawsuit.

And might this have been known to Peters and Waterman (1982)? We cannot of course answer this question definitively. Nonetheless, we suggest that it would surely take some effort for two individuals operating as 'partners' within one of the world's leading business consulting organizations to be wholly unaware of Bechtel's widely publicized and growing legal problems! Indeed, Denton (2016: 120) reminds us that even as the class action suits brought by its black and female employees progressed through the court system

> Bechtel was . . . being pummelled by a sudden, unfamiliar and relentless bad publicity. *The Washington Star* had been running an investigative series of articles about Bechtel's business practices, its ties to government agencies, and its uncanny ability to obtain no-bid contracts. Then there was the bribery scheme involving a pipeline right-of-way in New Jersey that led to the convictions of four Bechtel employees.

The indictment of six Bechtel employees at Calvert Cliffs, Maryland, nuclear plant, charged with extorting nearly a quarter of a million dollars, followed.

Placing this appreciation of Bechtel within the context of *In Search of Excellence,* it should now be apparent that the company's secretive practices simply denied Peters and Waterman (1982) the intelligence necessary to validate their core assertion. Frankly the authors did not know and could not know if Bechtel was, on the six indicators selected, truly performing beyond its peers. Furthermore, the company's obsession with secrecy all but prevented the authors from exploring the extent to which the Bechtel's success was truthfully dependent upon its commitment to the eight organizational attributes, said to underpin business excellence. But some things *were* known. It was known that the company discriminated against its black employees, against its female employees and against those of the Jewish faith. In addition, it was known that the company had been involved in bribery and corruption. Any one of these widely-reported controversies, we suggest, should have been enough to deny Bechtel its exemplary status. Yet, somehow these reports *either* slipped under the radar of the research undertaken by Peters and Waterman (1982) *or worse* . . . were known to the authors but were deemed to be somehow, routine, normal and inconsequential to the larger excellence project. Whatever the case, Bechtel while conspicuously successful is, we suggest it is a rather poor exemplar for a system of management that is said to be customer-focused and driven by a clear set of cultural values that celebrate the virtues of fairness and open-ness!

Boeing

The company made famous by its 747 'jumbo jet' (and perhaps infamous by its B52) was founded by William Boeing and two very junior partners, Edgar Goff and James Foley on July 15, 1916 when powered flight was still in its infancy (Pelletier [2008] 2010: 14).[5] On May 9, 1917 the company, which had originally been incorporated as The Pacific Aero Products Company, took the name of its founder and became The Boeing Airline Company.

It would be fair to say that in its early years, and at key points in its history, Boeing has struggled to keep afloat and has, as Pelletier ([2008] 2010: 17) notes, 'remained in business thanks to orders from the US Army.' This is not to suggest of course that Boeing has failed to innovate or has in any sense been complacent in the face of challenges posed, variously, by competitors and technological innovation. Indeed it is worth observing that the company was very much a pioneer in the field of commercial passenger transport, having made adaptations to its mail-carrying aircraft to accommodate, however modestly, a paying passenger. Indeed it was a scandal around the award of such mail contracts and a subsequent, legally-mandated instruction to break up the co-operative relationships that had been brokered between the aircraft construction companies and the nascent airlines that, in 1934, caused William Boeing to walk out on the company that he had founded and so carefully nurtured.

The changes, mandated within the industry in the early 1930s caused significant problems for *Boeing* during this period. In response the company chose to make significant cuts to its workforce; placing those who retained their employment on part-time working. By the late 1930s, however, things were once again looking brighter for the company, and while *Boeing* initially lost out to competitors who had developed designs for 'fighter' aircraft, its B17 bomber soon became central to America's war strategy.

In the post-war period Boeing continued to design aircraft for the military, producing for example, the B52 bomber, which was used with devastating effect in Vietnam, Laos and Cambodia. It is said that the initial design for this long-lived and iconic aircraft was conceived in a hotel room and took just a matter of hours to produce (Pelletier [2008] 2010: 118). This 'genesis narrative' may be broadly truthful. Yet, it is worth noting that while the tale of the B52's origins is plainly attractive as a sense-giving device (see Collins, 2018, 2022), the mythology does tend to overlook the 11.5 million hours that Boeing's staff devoted to refining the design and to prototyping and testing the aircraft (Pelletier [2008] 2010: 121).

During the early post-war period, Boeing also began to develop a series of commercial airliners and related military (tanker) variants to supplement its military contracts. The first of these commercial aircraft, the 707, was prototyped in 1954 and was followed by a series of truly remarkable aircraft: the 727; the 737 and the 747 in 1968. Reflecting this shifting product range and its increasing diversification beyond the aviation market, the company chose, once again, to change its name and became The Boeing Company in 1961. In December 1972 the re-named company was restructured into three autonomous units, the first devoted to commercial aircraft, the second to military products, with the third offering a wider portfolio of activities which over the next few years would see The Boeing Company branch out into computing, construction and related maintenance services. Yet, despite the success of its 747 'jumbo' jet, the early 1970s proved to be another difficult period for the company. A reduction in military expenditure associated with the withdrawal of American forces from Vietnam, the shrinkage of the Apollo space programme, for which Boeing had provided the space buggy amongst other components, and the colossal investment required to meet customer demand for the 747 caused profit to fall to $10 million in

1969 (Pelletier [2008] 2010: 171). When the order book for the 747 col-
lapsed soon afterwards, Boeing once again chose to cut its workforce. In the
four years between 1967 and 1971, headcount within the company fell from
100,874 to just 53,300. In 1972, however, the company's fortunes improved
once more. Boeing was able to increase recruitment again and, by 1980 the
company's payroll, had reached a new peak of 113, 172 (Pelletier [2008]
2010: 171).

It is, we suggest, difficult to imagine that a company with Boeing's
volatile past and with its history of 'hire and fire' could be characterized
as a leading financial performer over the extended time-period preferred
by Peters and Waterman (1982). Yet, despite this reservation, it would be
fair to suggest that the company *had* been a key part of an endeavour that
had genuinely revolutionized aircraft production during the war years.
Furthermore we must concede that Boeing has been a consistent innovator
and has (very much as Peters and Waterman advised) developed a mythology to project and to account for this activity. Beyond such mythology
however, it may be helpful to observe that Boeing did in fact take a very
significant commercial risk when it offered the 727 to its customers for it
chose to skip the normal prototyping process and moved, directly from the
design to the production phase of the project! Furthermore, the company
had, in an attempt to overcome the advantages enjoyed by key competitors
such as Lockheed, worked very hard to get close to its customers, offering
the 707, for example, in a bewildering number of (not very cost-effective)
variants.

And yet, while Boeing does seem to exhibit some of the attributes
that Peters and Waterman have suggested are characteristic of business
excellence, the company has also engaged in activities that surely tar-
nish its reputation as a beacon for managerial practice. Sampson's (1977)
widely-read account of the arms industry, which was published just as the
research for the excellence project was commencing, for example, documents a complex web of intrigue and state-sponsored corruption which
implicates Boeing. To be fair to the company, we should concede that
Boeing appears to have been but a bit-player within an arena notable
for dodgy dealing which had seen Lockheed – with the approval of the
Executive Branch in Washington – make corrupt(ing) payments to mid-
dlemen of $2.25 million in order to secure a foothold in the Japanese
civilian aviation market (Sampson, 1977: 227–228). Nonetheless, while
Boeing may have been a minor player in this corruption, it *did* become
involved in corrupt activities and was, while wrestling with what Pelletier
([2008] 2010: 126) terms the 'cut-throat battle for market share,' willing
to indulge bribery. Discussing Boeing's dealings in the Japanese market,
Sampson (1977: 228) notes:

Boeing was looked after by the Nissho-Iwai Trading Company, to which Boeing was later found to have made large "improper payments."

Peters and Waterman (1982), putative experts in the business of management, make no mention of this. This omission is curious and more than a little alarming. It suggests that the authors either deliberately chose to exclude their knowledge of the realities of business practice from their account of business excellence or were rather naïve observers of the corporate estate. Frankly we are unsure which of these explanations is more alarming. Yet, whatever the truth of the situation the reality is that Peters and Waterman did not (or could not) share what Sampson (1977) knew to be true – that an element of the business success enjoyed by *Boeing* was a result of knavery on a pretty large scale!

Caterpillar

Woolfson and Foster (1988: 4) describe Caterpillar as 'a fairly typical American firm.' Expanding upon this declaration, however, they concede that it was perhaps unusual in at least one respect: its success:

It grew faster than most. It had somewhat more (20 per cent) of its productive resources outside the United States. It was involved in a production area at the heavier, less electronic end of the technological spectrum. But as the tenth largest US industrial exporter and at place 52 in the Fortune 500 of top US firms, it would have seemed a prime example of crisis-free technological excellence, and, as its directors claimed, living proof that the free market system combined maximum prosperity with human dignity.

(4)

Certainly the official company history carefully prepared by Caterpillar Inc (as the company is now known) offers an account of the development of the organization, which suggests that Caterpillar has invested heavily in technology and its people and, in so doing, has very much enjoyed a crisis-free existence.[6] In their account of the factory occupation organized as an attempt to prevent the planned closure of Caterpillar's Uddingston (Scotland) plant, Woolfson and Foster (1988) offer a potted history of the company that contrasts sharply with that preferred by Caterpillar's corporate communications office. Indeed, we should note that the history offered by Woolfson and Foster offers a useful and distinctive piece of historiography for it eschews the normal tropes of corporate biography/

hagiography in favour of an analysis rooted in political economy. Thus, where Caterpillar's official history celebrates vision, foresight and technological advance, Woolfson and Foster offer an analysis of action-in-context which allows us to consider the condition and possibilities of managerial endeavour.

At one level, Caterpillar is we should concede an unpromising subject for a (corporate) biography. It lacks what we might term 'the humble origins narrative' that is preferred by *hacks* and by the laureates of the corporate world who write for publications such as *Harvard Business Review*. Indeed Woolfson and Foster are clear that Caterpillar started out big. The company was, from the outset, the largest farm equipment producer in the US because it brought together two existing companies, *Holt* and *C L Best*, which between them dominated the US home market for powered agricultural equipment. Caterpillar's official history acknowledges this fact of course but in keeping with its preferred narrative approach glosses over the specifics of the merger, choosing to credit this to *the vision* of Harry Fair who served on the company's Board of Directors from 1925 until 1954. There is, however, space for a less sanitized account of this merger. Indeed it may be useful to note that both *Holt* and *C L Best* had struggled through the depression years of 1920–1921 and were, in effect, obliged to merge by investors who had become concerned that the value of their shareholdings was being squandered by mutually destructive contractual, trademark and patent law infringement law-suits which had since 1905 consumed some $1.5 million (a sum in excess of $22 million at today's prices).[7]

Noting the formation of the Caterpillar Tractor Company in 1925[8] 'Company-Histories'[9] challenges the crisis-free narrative preferred by the official company history. It notes for example that from 1961 the company suffered a series of labour disputes. Indeed this source hints that the joint venture with Mitsubishi, launched in 1963 was, in part, an attempt to secure production within a more compliant labour-management context. Whatever the rationale for the Japanese joint venture it is plain that throughout the post-war period Caterpillar's apparently crisis-free existence was, in fact, punctuated by a series of protracted labour disputes in (for example) 1964, 1966 and 1979. This latter dispute, which involved 23,000 workers and which took more than three months to resolve, was especially disruptive for Caterpillar because it caused parts shortages across the estate which obliged the company to lay-off 3,500 workers. Yet, none of this features in the official history preferred by Caterpillar, nor does it intrude upon the narrative developed by Peters and Waterman (1982).

We should concede, of course, that aspects of Caterpillar's preferred historical narrative are truthful at root. The company has, for example, made significant technological innovations. Woolfson and Foster (1988) acknowledge this although their potted history tends to focus only upon the achievements of Holt. Thus, Woolfson and Foster note that Holt developed the prototype for a petrol-driven, tracked vehicle in 1908. This prototype, we should note, would later form the platform for the armoured 'tanks' which the British military employed on the battlefields of France in 1916. In the 1920s Holt pioneered the application of diesel technology in tractor units and broadened its product range to include earth-moving and construction equipment. In time, the authors observe, Caterpillar would itself become a supplier of diesel power units for other manufacturers and grew rapidly when it won the contract to supply diesel engines for the US military's M4 tank.

In the immediate post-war period, Caterpillar rapidly transformed. It leveraged the cost-advantages arising from its domination of the domestic market to become a major exporter. During the 1950s, however, having successfully dislodged indigenous producers, Caterpillar moved from being, simply, an exporter to become a fully-fledged multi-national company with plants in England (1950), Brazil (1954), Australia (1955), Canada (1956), France (1956), Mexico (1962), India (1962) and Belgium (1965) (Woolfson and Foster, 1988: 2). Commenting upon this growth strategy, Woolfson and Foster (1988: 3) suggest that it was a direct product of the strength of the US currency, which in being tied to the value of gold allowed organizations such as Caterpillar 'to buy up vast slabs of raw materials, oil, uranium, copper at knock down prices.' Yet, Woolfson and Foster (1988: 3) observe that while the strength of the US dollar conferred distinct advantages for Caterpillar it also reduced the profitability of US exports and in so doing encouraged the company to 'produce . . . goods abroad and repatriate the profits.'

Woolfson and Foster (1988) offer a useful exploration of these economic movements and their impacts throughout the 1970s and early 1980s. Indeed the authors highlight growing problems for Caterpillar and a developing sense of crisis within and beyond the company. Yet where Peters and Waterman reduce (1982) this crisis to a problem with roots in 'culture,' Woolfson and Foster trace the manner in which geo-political shifts set the conditions for American managerial action during these turbulent decades. Thus, they highlight three key issues for Caterpillar.

The first of these issues, they suggest, arose in the 1970s as a consequence of changes in the management of the European Economic Community (EEC), the development of protectionist trade policy in Japan and the spread of new production techniques across the Japanese economy (especially those rooted in sub-contracting arrangements). Woolfson and Foster note that these developments led to an erosion of the economic advantages previously enjoyed by US producers. This US economic advantage was further eroded in the 1980s by a significant depreciation in the value of the Japanese Yen which made Japanese exports cheaper.

The second source of problems highlighted by Woolfson and Foster (1988) relates to what was known as the 'third world debt crisis' in the 1980s. In the decades prior to the 1980s the world's developed economies had allowed the Third World (now more commonly labelled as 'under-developed' or 'developing') economies to borrow substantial sums of money. In the 1980s, however, economic conditions changed – the inflation rate fell while interest rates rose. These movements caused a substantial rise in the real value of the debt owed by the Third World economies. This increasing debt burden precipitated short-run advantages for First-World corporations, a reduction in commodity prices *and* longer-term problems and the effective collapse of demand for Caterpillar's products within the developing economies.

The third source of problems identified by Woolfson and Foster (1988) relates to what the authors term the loss of US market dominance. The growing balance-of-payments deficit endured by the US economy is often cited as a key symptom of this economic shift. Yet, it would be more sensible to suggest that it was the 'monetarist' economic policies, applied to combat inflation, which generated significant problems for companies such as Caterpillar. Thus the application of 'monetarist' economic policies within the US caused a rise in domestic interest rates, and in so doing, precipitated a significant appreciation in the value of the dollar. This change in the relative value of the dollar reduced demand for US goods significantly because it made American exports prohibitively expensive for those developing countries already burdened by very high levels of debt.

Highlighting the consequences of these issues for Caterpillar, Woolfson and Foster (1988: 6–7) observe that between 1978 and 1984 the company's share of the market for earth-moving equipment declined from 44% to 35%. Indeed, 1982 (the year in which *In Search of Excellence* was first published) was a particularly bad year for the company. In this year, *Caterpillar's* overseas sales fell by 40%. *The Los Angeles Times* (13/01/1985) reports that this decline continued into 1984. Caterpillar, the paper observes, lost $180 million in 1982, $345 million in 1983 and $177 million in the first nine months of 1984. Putting the situation perhaps more plainly, Selko (2013) observes that during the early 1980s Caterpillar was, at times, haemorrhaging $1 million per day!

Within 'popular management' circumstances such as these are typically presented as a prompt to radical change management. Indeed such circumstances are often said to herald the arrival of a new and charismatic leader with a mandate to secure a turnaround through a shared vision, designed to engender a renewed sense of purpose throughout the organization. Woolfson and Foster (1988), however, reject this narrative. They proceed from a position that is, at once, more grounded and yet more abstract. They remind us that US corporations (especially) are slaves to the quarterly reporting cycle and are, in fact, beholden to the large financial institutions which own their shares. Recognizing this, Foster and Woolfson suggest that whatever the preferred narrative of 'popular management' might suggest, it was the major financial institutions who, in the final analysis demanded change from Caterpillar's management.

As the company began to craft what we would now term a turnaround strategy it was the US plants which were initially vulnerable. Thus, Caterpillar's management sought real terms wage cuts, a reduction in the value of the benefits package, and significant changes to working practices. US workers who had experienced declining real wages throughout the 1970s opposed these changes, however, and with the support of the UAW took strike action. This dispute took 205 days to resolve and was settled only when management withdrew most of their original demands. Nonetheless, Caterpillar did close two US plants in 1983 and a further two plants in 1984, moving production abroad (Woolfson and Foster, 1988).

In 1984 the economic fortunes of Caterpillar began to improve. Yet, Woolfson and Foster (1988: 8) suggest that this change is less the outcome of managerial vision and commitment and more the product of the 40% depreciation in the value of the dollar which made US exports attractive once more. This shift in currency values would, temporarily spare US workers from further upheaval. Now overseas plants such as that located in Uddingston, Scotland would become targets for closure.

Elaborating upon the manner in which Caterpillar has sought to manage its global workforce, Woolfson and Foster (1988) remind us that the (grudging commitment to) pluralism that underpins union-management relations in the US should be considered exceptional in this context because throughout the 1980s the company worked carefully to exclude trades unions from plants located in Brazil, Mexico and Indonesia. Probing further the values of a company that opportunistically denies certain groups access to representative structures of decision-making, Woolfson and Foster challenge directly the suggestion that Caterpillar is a model corporate citizen, an exemplar of 'hands-on; value-driven' management. For example, they observe that Caterpillar maintained a South African plant throughout the apartheid years, and in so doing, remind us that Caterpillar's value system was, apparently, not at all offended by a regime that was openly and explicitly racist! Turning their attention to the European operations of the company, Woolfson and Foster (1988) observe that despite testimonials as to the open nature of its communications, Caterpillar was happy to work with the Thatcher government in the UK to block proposals, which would have granted trades unions access to company information on corporate plans including those related to plant closures.

As we close this case report it will be useful to observe that Caterpillar's own account of its history reminds us that, in 1970, the company's sales beyond the US exceeded those earned within America for the first time. Despite this global expansion and reach, however, the company has been keen to stress that no matter their location the expectations placed upon employees remain the same; we are reassured that employees the world over are expected to pursue excellence in all that they do. What our analysis of Caterpillar has demonstrated is an absence of reciprocity in this relationship which in practice suggests that while the company is plainly driven by a set of values, its core tenets and standard operating practices are not, in truth, the wholesome, plain truths suggested within the covers of *In Search of Excellence*. Indeed our analysis of the company's conduct suggests that its values are complex, capricious and shaped not so much by a stable moral code but by opportunism. Or, more plainly, the analysis of Woolfson and Foster (1988) suggests the presence of intervening variables, which shape the company's values-in-action. Prominent among these intervening variables is it seems melanin!

Dana

The company now known as Dana International was founded by Clarence Spicer in Plainfield, New Jersey in the year 1904 to manufacture universal joints – coupling devices that transmit rotary motion from one shaft to another. In later years the company widened its product range beyond the drive-train to supply a diverse range of automotive components to the automobile industry and to what is known as the 'after-market' industry. Despite the innovative engineering of Clarence Spicer, the company – then, named the *Spicer Manufacturing Company* – found itself in financial difficulties just a decade after its formation. Charles Dana, an attorney, became company president in 1916 and soon after made a significant personal investment in the organization. The company relocated to Toledo, Ohio in 1928 and in 1946 became the Dana Corporation. Charles Dana was subsequently named chairman in 1948. A series of acquisitions in this post-war period brought the company considerable financial success.

In the late 1960s Rene McPherson, who features prominently in the writing of Tom Peters (see Collins, 2022) was appointed company president. McPherson quickly implemented a number of sweeping changes within *Dana*. Famously he cut 350 people from the staff of 500, located within corporate headquarters (Berlin, 1986). In addition he shredded the company's stack of operating manuals, which, depending upon who you ask is said, variously, to have stood at 17.5 inches tall (see Berlin, 1986) or 22.5 inches in height (Hayes, 1979), in favour of a simple, brief policy statement. It may be useful to observe however that the fate of those 350 employees deemed superfluous by McPherson never seems to trouble Peters and Waterman (1982). This silence gives clues as to the extent to which the values, said to be central to the excellence project are, in truth, sustainable and indeed reciprocal!

More positively we should, of course, observe that when not slashing his corporate headquarters, McPherson did take time to institute an employee stock ownership scheme built around what has come to be known as the Scanlon Plan. In a controversial development McPherson also abolished the traditional form of factory discipline and control known as 'clocking-in' and was, publicly at least, unconcerned by any statutory issues arising in this context (see Collins, 2022).

Thanks, in part, to McPherson's distinctive managerial style, *Dana* had by the 1970s become a much-admired company. By the early 1980s, it had been celebrated by Peters and Waterman (1982) as exemplifying the organizational attributes said to be necessary for business excellence. Yet, while it is important to acknowledge the distinctive nature of McPherson's managerial approach we should not assume that his successes were clearly or narrowly attributable to his adherence to the attributes of excellence outlined by Peters and Waterman. Indeed, it is abundantly clear that Rene McPherson certainly did not 'stick to the knitting.' Between 1963 and 1980 (when McPherson retired to become the Dean of Stanford's Business School), Dana acquired 24 companies beyond the organization's original vehicle equipment business. It is these acquisitions which were associated with a transformation in *Dana's* profitability with profits rising from $62 million in 1975 to $164 million in 1979.[10] This lucrative programme of diversification continued into the 1980s when *Dana* made acquisitions in the financial services industry.

Despite these acquisitions, Dana encountered serious difficulties in the 1980s. These problems may be traced back to the 1970s when the company made a bet as to consumer preferences, and in so doing, chose to focus upon the manufacture of 'light truck' parts. Unfortunately, consumer preferences shifted away from light trucks in the 1980s, and the company experienced a significant reduction in demand. Indeed between 1980 and 1982 the company suffered an almost 50% reduction in earnings. In response to this developing crisis, Dana closed five US plants and laid off one third of its US employees. Unlike other organizations the company made wholesale lay-offs in this period, however, Dana seems to have helped (former) employees to find alternative employment and indeed offered some assistance with relocation expenses. This is, of course, commendable but we must not lose sight of one rather uncomfortable fact: Dana's production process, and indeed its products, have killed many of its employees and many of its customers. This situation arises because so many of the products that Dana manufactured contained asbestos. Indeed as the toxic effects of asbestos have become understood the company has found itself facing liability claims. In 2005, for example, it defended some 28,000 actions.

Dana precipitated controversy among its employees and raised difficult questions as to the nature of its core values when it filed for Chapter 11 bankruptcy in 2006. Indeed it was claimed that Dana was seeking to evade its economic (and moral) obligations to those it had harmed. Despite these complaints the reorganization plan was approved in late 2007 and, at this point, the company established Dana Companies LLC, a wholly-owned subsidiary to hold and to manage the asbestos claims which had by then begun to arrive in volume. In October of that year the company resolved 7,500 from a total of 150,000 outstanding asbestos claims with a $2 million settlement. In addition, Dana offered the reassurance that it had insured against further claims and had set aside $240 million in cash and other assets to cover future liabilities. To give some understanding of the extent of these liabilities, it may be useful to note that in 2010 Dana estimated that its exposure to asbestos-related liabilities would extend into 2025.

Since its reorganization in 2007, Dana has once again sought to acquire new businesses. These acquisitions have extended the company's product range, which now includes electric drivetrains for the automobile industry. Today Dana is headquartered in Maumee, Ohio and employs around 36,000 people. In 2020, the company's total assets were reported as $7.1 billion.

Rene McPherson, we should note, was celebrated by Peters and Waterman (1982) for his vision and for his willingness to shred bureaucracy. We have, of course, suggested that *In Search of Excellence* has been, at times, rather glib about the fate of those employees who find themselves drawn into the corporate shredder. Nevertheless, and in contrast to our first two case reports, there is no evidence to suggest that McPherson and the company he led were anything other than law-abiding. Yet we must not forget that Dana's actions have killed customers and employees. We should not forget that in the face of growing litigation Dana (with assets valued in excess of $7 billion) has been obliged to place the interests of its stockholders above those of its other stakeholders – its employees, former employees and customers – and has consequently used every resource at its disposal to defend itself against legal actions brought by those seeking some small redress for their suffering.

Delta Airlines

Offering an outline of the practices and priorities that shaped the constitution of their panel of excellent organizations, Peters and Waterman (1982) paused to inform their readers that they had chosen to exclude banking from their analytical frame. The peculiarities of this highly regulated context, they reasoned, made banking a special case, a useful subject for later, and more detailed consideration of business excellence. This is, we acknowledge, a reasonable point. Context does indeed matter (Pettigrew, 1985). Yet, this formal (if incomplete) acknowledgement of the manner in which context shapes and is shaped by managerial action does not explain why Johnson & Johnson, a supplier of medicines and related pharmaceuticals and hence closely regulated by the Food and Drugs Administration (FDA), made the cut. Nor does it explain why Delta Airlines, operating within perhaps one of the most heavily regulated sectors of the economy, merits inclusion as an exemplary model of business excellence!

Of course there is a fairly simple explanation for the inclusion of Delta. This explanation, however, relates not to the consideration of contextual variables and market vagaries but to narrative preferences. The work of Peters and Waterman (1982), you see, displays clear narrative preferences. While others may protest that organizational structure and function must be located within narratives that embed these aspects of our lives in a properly contextual-historical fashion (see Pettigrew for a classic rendering of this position), Peters and Waterman seem to believe that the corporate world is best rendered in, and through, heroic narratives (see Collins, 2007, 2022). These narratives while variously amusing and edifying however, tend to adopt a reductionist stance as regards the complex realities of corporate endeavour (and success). Thus, where Pettigrew (1985) examines the manner in which context and action interact to develop complex and cumulating priorities, Peters and Waterman choose a simpler narrative which suggests that business excellence is a product of the vision and resilience of a small handful of truly remarkable individuals. Reflecting these priorities and presuppositions, the narrative of Delta Airlines preferred by Peters and Waterman (1982) ignores the peculiarities of the company's operating context in favour of a celebration of C E Woolman, the man who would dominate Delta Airlines for 40 years. Yet this narrative retains one fundamental flaw: it simply denies the reader any meaningful understanding of the company and so fails to deliver the 'lessons' on the business of management that Peters and Waterman (1982) promised their readers.

Offering a history of *Delta Airlines* Lewis and Newton [1979] (2016) provide a useful biography of C E Woolman, which invites us to explore the dynamic complexities of the US airline industry. Woolman, we are told, was born in 1889 and graduated with a degree in agriculture in 1912. His first job after graduation was as the manager of a 7,000-acre plantation in Louisiana. However a keen interest in aviation led Woolman to join a crop-dusting operation known as Duff Haland in 1925. Yet, Woolman did not join as a pilot. He was, in fact, hired to develop the procedures necessary to allow the company to improve the management of its contract negotiations and employee evaluations.

In 1926, Duff Haland expanded its operations to capitalize on the growing market for airmail and passenger transport and became the Keystone Aircraft Corporation. A crop-spraying operation was retained by *Keystone* but this was hived off to a separate division to be known as Duff Haland Dusters. Following this divisionalization, the company expanded into Peru, offering its services to an agricultural sector, which because it had a significant cotton crop often required the application of pesticides. Given our earlier comments regarding the importance of context, however, it will be useful to observe that this Peruvian expansion was assisted by the US State Department, which due to growing concerns regarding a) European influence in South America and b) the security of the Panama Canal was keen to establish a stronger US presence in the region.

The Keystone Aircraft Corporation, which had by now been purchased by a group of Wall Street investors, instructed Woolman to expand company operations within Peru. Woolman duly submitted a bid to provide airmail and passenger transport within this territory. The company was successful in this endeavour. Yet, in choosing to focus upon the mail delivery element of its business, Keystone decided to divest its crop-dusting division. Woolman, apparently keen to branch out on his own, agreed to purchase Huff Daland Dusters, renaming it Delta Airline Service Inc. This new company carried its first passengers on June 17, 1929 (the date which Lewis and Newton [1979] (2006) choose as the effective birth of Delta).

Delta Airline Service Inc. prospered initially by offering a combination of crop-dusting, airmail and passenger services. Indeed by 1930, the company was offering regular, scheduled flights. Yet, soon after this date the company suffered a significant set-back when it lost out on the government-run bidding process to provide airmail services within the US. As a consequence of being, in effect, locked out of the US airmail business, the company was forced to fall back on its crop-dusting service. Indeed, Lewis and Newton suggest that the company lived hand-to-mouth during the early 1930s and only survived the first half of the decade thanks to the leadership of Woolman whom they characterize as genial, paternalistic and financially conservative. By the mid-1930s, however, the company's fortunes began to improve. The US government had commissioned an inquiry into the process used to award airmail contracts and decided that this had not been executed lawfully. Delta, which had been treated very unfairly duly re-entered the bidding process, was awarded one of the airmail routes and used this platform to rebuild its business.

By the mid-1970s, as Peters and Waterman (1982) began to prepare their account of business excellence Delta was a very successful and we should note a very highly-regarded US carrier. Documenting the company's growth and indeed its growing reputation, Lewis and Newton [1979] (2016: 393) observe that between 1972 and 1978 Delta increased its revenues from $883.5 million to $1.7 billion, as passenger numbers rose from 20.5 million to 28.8 million. We should note, however, that figures for the 'emplanement' of passengers are inflated by regulatory requirements which denied the company the right to make direct flights to key destinations and so obliged passengers to change at key hubs (such as Atlanta) before moving on to their final destination.

In 1978, company profits exceeded $100 million for the first time. Furthermore, Delta had been recognized as an industry leader having secured a reliability rate of 99.28% on its scheduled flights. These figures are all the more impressive given the steep rise in fuel prices in the early 1970s and the recession of 1975, which had obliged the company to overhaul its fleet in order to secure greater fuel efficiency.

Peters and Waterman (1982) make just eight direct references to Delta Airlines. The authors offer a very brief, potted history of the company that observes recent deregulation within the industry (253–255) and build upon this to highlight the company's 'family feeling' (103; 283) and its open-door management policy (122). In addition, the authors celebrate the informality that characterizes its senior management meetings (219; 290), while noting the company's envied reputation for reliability and punctuality (179; 191). All of this we are assured is a product of 'culture' and may be traced back to the 'leadership' of the company's top management team. However, do such vignettes amount to lessons on business that might be used to develop excellent outcomes elsewhere in the airline business? Beyond exhortation, do such tales of flexibility and, apparently, open communications offer a) a meaningful appreciation of what it means to work for Delta and do they b) provide something (*anything!*) that the reader might use to build business success in this or indeed in any other arena? Hardly. Indeed the truth is that Peters and Waterman (1982) demonstrate a serious lack of curiosity when it comes to the wider context of Delta's operations and success. Perhaps it was just too difficult to account for the company's early sponsorship by the State Department and its unlawful exclusion from government contracts within a celebration of America's vaunted free market system, but the truth is that Delta's successes (and setbacks) need to be understood within this context.

There is a joke that is often made at Delta's expense, which highlights the extent to which the company uses a 'hub and spokes' system to manage its scheduled operations. This joke suggests that after death, whether you are headed for heaven or bound for hell, you will be obliged to change at Atlanta (Lewis and Newton [1979] 2016: 398). What Peters and Waterman (1982) fail to acknowledge, of course, is that the hub and spoke system, to which this joke refers, was an expedient response to a constraint set by regulators who in weighing up the merits of competition had denied *Delta* the right to make direct flights to key destinations. Furthermore we should acknowledge that until 1977 when the company was finally permitted to offer flights between Atlanta and London, *Delta* had been restricted to domestic operations thanks to the regulation of international routes and airport take-off slots.

Of course Peters and Waterman (1982) do acknowledge recent deregulation within the airline industry. Deregulation does not amount to the absence of regulation. And the truth is that Delta had become a leading organization within a complex and highly regulated business. Indeed the company's successes arose due to its ability to manage through and within these processes. But we hear nothing of this within the covers of *In Search of Excellence*.

So what may be said of Delta's management approach and style? Peters and Waterman (1982) place a lot of weight on the manner in which *Delta's* management organized its communications. Flexibility, informality and open-ness had developed a meaningful 'family feeling' within a large, complex and geographically diverse organization. But this familial metaphor, while highlighting notions of commonality and consensus, also makes space for other less wholesome elements of family life, which invite us to consider direction, control and sometimes simple coercion.

Explaining its preference for an operating environment free from collective agreements Delta Airlines insists that it is, in fact, 'pro-people' (Lewis and Newton [1979] 2016: 400). This is an interesting rhetorical flourish. What right-minded individual could be 'anti-people'?

Yet Delta's 'pro-people' policy is, of course, simultaneously 'anti-democracy' insofar as it has been designed to prevent the formation of the voluntary social collectives (more commonly known as unions) which workers organize to secure a voice in those organizational processes that have a material impact upon their lives and upon their communities! Commenting upon the company's industrial relations climate, Peters and Waterman (1982: 253) develop a sudden interest in matters historical. Delta they observe, has not suffered a strike since 1942. What they fail to acknowledge and what they fail to provide as a meaningful lesson for their readers is the understanding that this strike-free environment is the product of a strategic choice. Thus, we should note that Delta's pro-people/anti-unionism approach led the company to develop a 'high road' employee relations strategy. This distinctive strategic approach opposes unionization by reducing the incentive for union membership. In short a 'high road' employee relations strategy voluntarily provides terms and conditions that are at least on a par with those that in other circumstances union officials would need to wrest as concessions from management. This approach is, of course, commendable and does contrast with the 'low road' strategy that has been utilised by *Emerson*. Nonetheless, it is worth pointing out that *Delta's* pro-people managerial approach is anti-democratic; it is a product of the broader context ignored by Peters and Waterman and is, of course, contingent upon the presence of viable trade union structures and policies elsewhere in the economy.

This is not to suggest, of course, that Delta's management is entirely lacking in social conscience. Indeed we should note that the company – partly as a response to staff shortages (Lewis and Newton [1979] 2016: 402–403) – was an active advocate for 'affirmative action' programmes, which sought to improve the employment outcomes for minorities and for the long-term unemployed. However, we should not allow this activity to blind us to the broader context of family life which we hinted at above.

Throughout the 1970s – when Peters and Waterman (1982) were apparently researching the company in some depth – Delta was regularly involved in litigation as it demanded the right to impose dress codes and regular weight checks on its cabin crew employees. Lewis and Newton ([1979] 2016) observe that the company cited safety concerns in its submissions to the courts and was generally successful in the defence of its actions and policies. But that is hardly the point. It is surely a curious and unwholesome sort of family that reserves the right to dictate the shape and size of its female members *and* their clothing!

That said our case report on Delta Airlines is rather unlike the reports we have offered on Fluor, Bechtel and Boeing (to cite just three examples). Our case report, for example, offers no evidence of widespread bribery and corruption. Nor is there evidence of the systematic abuse of staff, which as we shall see was evident within Procter and Gamble and to a lesser extent Emerson. Indeed our reflections suggest that *Delta* has, at key points, been a victim of the knavery of others!

Yet, what our case report does uncover is a stunning lack of curiosity on the part of Peters and Waterman (1982): a failure to provide any meaningful insight on the context of Delta's operations and, consequently, few if any lessons on the day-to-day dilemmas and complexities of business that a would-be manager might actually implement. Readers, of course, may well protest that Peters was himself aware of just this limitation and so published *A Passion for Excellence* (Peters and Austin, 1985) to provide guidance on the implementation challenges associated with the excellence project. This is, of course, true to some extent. Peters and Austin (1985) did indeed offer their book as a guide to 'implementation.' Yet, if anything this follow-up work is even more reductionist than its predecessor insofar as it seems to reduce the totality of the excellence project to just two variables – customers and innovation (Collins, 2000, 2007, 2022) – and in so doing, simply assumes away the contextual facilitators and constraints that have shaped the operation of Delta Airlines. Indeed this tendency to assume away problems and constraints may be the ultimate tragedy of the narrative preferred by Peters and Waterman (1982) for in overlooking the complexities associated with Delta's operations, the authors actually diminish their heroes, and in so doing prevent us from understanding the managerial problems; the geo-political processes, trade-offs, leaps-of-faith and dumb luck that shape business. In other words and despite the promise of 'lessons' that may be learned, the account of *Delta Airlines* offered by Peters and Waterman (1982) simply fails to understand and in so doing fails to communicate in any meaningful way just what it takes to succeed in the airline business.

Digital Equipment

Digital Equipment Corporation was founded in 1957 by Ken Olsen and Harland Anderson with $70,000 seed-funding provided by the venture capitalist organization American Research & Development. Olsen and Harland had been warned that they should not pitch their venture as 'a computer business,' and so they focused their plans on the provision of printed circuit boards. Digital we should note was successful in this endeavour from the outset, shipping $94,000 worth of product and posting a profit in its first year of operation.

In 1960 the company produced its first computer, the PDP-1 (an abbreviation of Program Data Processor). Unusually for the time this computer was delivered with a visual display unit which allowed the user to directly review their inputs to the processor. Where the mainframe computers of this period were room-sized and retailed for around $1 million, the PDP-1 was distinctive. It was the size of a domestic refrigerator, cost just $180,000 and, of course, had a direct user interface. The PDP-1 was, in time, followed by later variants priced between $27,000 and $300,000 (for the PDP-6).

While pursuing a distinctive technological strategy, Digital also developed organizational processes that were unusual within this emerging industry. Where IBM leased its equipment and developed a large bureaucratic organization to manage the sale of consumables to users who were largely ignorant of the technology and so highly dependent upon the vendor, Digital Equipment Corporation deliberately maintained *ad hoc* organizational arrangements and chose to sell to scientists and engineers who were themselves capable of managing and maintaining the equipment. Indeed it is worth noting that other vendors often purchased Digital technology, before adding their own proprietary software and packaging this new bundle as their own product.

Historians of Digital Equipment Corporation generally suggest that the *ad hoc* organizational arrangements, which characterized Digital's operations in its early years, were called into question by product delays, which by the mid-1960s were causing bottlenecks in the supply chain. To overcome these problems Digital developed an innovative approach. It chose a matrix organization designed, explicitly, to manage the control-innovation paradox that is central to the work of management and, of course, central to the excellence project.

Between 1965 and 1967 *Digital's* revenues increased six-fold and profitability grew at a similarly astronomical rate. Perhaps unsurprisingly, the company began to attract the attention of journalists and academics. The profiles developed at this time highlighted the company's no lay-off policy and what was said to be its culture of open communications.

Contemporary accounts of Digital Equipment Corporation, which was purchased by Compaq in 1998 before finding itself tied to Hewlett Packard in 2002, have been built upon attempts to explain why an organization that was once so successful and innovative should find itself humbled. Echoing the account of culture developed by Kroeber and Kluckhohn (1952), Schein (2003) deploys a biological metaphor to account for Digital's fall. He suggests that, while those leading the company should be acknowledged as innovators in the related fields of technology and organization, they simply lacked the 'gene' necessary to make their endeavours successful in business terms. Furthermore, he suggests that Digital simply failed to acknowledge the existence of *Moore's Law,*[11] which made it clear that the company would be unable to compete in a marketplace characterized by collapsing costs. In an appendix to Schein's (2003) text, Bell (2003) offers a dissenting viewpoint. Countering Schein's preferred narrative he argues that the company fell from grace because it was weighed down by a Board that was ignorant of the company's core technology, and so, failed to spot key opportunities in the market. In addition Bell complains that Digital was failed by incompetent managers who did not appreciate that their refusal to accommodate new industry standards and protocols would in effect secure Digital's exit from the marketplace.

Bell's counterpoint to Schein's analysis is interesting. Yet, while Bell disputes Schein's (2003) preferred resolution of the problem, his counter-narrative fails to challenge the larger suggestion that all companies need, and some companies may lack, a genetic disposition towards money-making.

Offering an overview of the, then, developing literature on cultures and organizations, Kroeber and Kluckhohn (1952) render a distinction between descriptive, historical, normative, psychological, structural and genetic accounts. Yet, where Schein's genetic appreciation of *Digital* suggests that business success is to be found in some corporate double-helix that predisposes some organizational forms to money-making, the 'genetic' appreciation of culture that is offered by Kroeber and Kluckhohn is rooted in a very human and deeply social form of analysis. Thus, for Kroeber and Kluckhohn, 'genetic' accounts of culture are said to turn upon a consideration of the human-made elements of our environment: the mental constructs that shape our explanatory schema, and the symbolic fabrication of those artefacts that we employ in our everyday interactions. Schein (2003), however, seems to have settled upon a profoundly asocial account of Digital's legacy. Indeed, while offering extended reflections on leadership, values and technology, and while praising Olsen for squaring the circle between espoused and lived 'values,' Schein seems to indulge a form of corporate eugenics, which in suggesting that some formations simply lack the biological make-up for business success makes room for an entrepreneurial superman who must take steps to prevent the *untermenschen*: the *oompa loompas* of technology from becoming welfare dependent.[12]

Schein's (2003) corporate eugenics is, of course, focused upon the organizational elite at the heart of Digital. As he attempts to explain the birth, growth and ultimate demise of this innovative organization he is naturally drawn to those within the corporate headquarters who made the key, high-level decisions. As we re-view Digital's legacy and its excellence (or otherwise) we will take a different path and a road less travelled. Thus, we turn our attention to those who have been written out of Schein's story and who have been cast from the excellence project. Thus, where Schein focuses upon the organization's leaders and architects, we will look towards the company's production facilities as we offer reflections on what it takes – and what it costs – to deliver upon the promise of *Moore's Law*.

Today almost all of us are obliged to interact with digital technologies. These technologies are, we should note, quite unlike their electromechanical precursors in that their inner workings are hidden from the user and are furthermore unknown to most. We seldom pause to consider what it might take to deliver the technologies that we now routinely employ. And that is perhaps just as well.

In 1986 Digital Equipment Corporation became aware of issues impacting upon those working in the 'clean rooms' that it had built to manufacture the components that lie at the heart of our digital technologies. It duly commissioned a small scientific study to explore this concern. To its credit, Digital agreed that the findings of this initial study, which demonstrated a link between the manufacture of semiconductors and spontaneous abortion, should be published (see Pastides et al., 1988). It is, however, worth observing that as early as 1982 the Semiconductor Industry Association had informed its members of the risks associated with dermal exposure to ethylene glycol ethers, had advocated minimizing the use of this chemical and, indeed, had recommended alternative solvents such as propylene glycol ethers. Most companies, however, took no action until 1995 when an industry study (see Schenker et al., 1995) was finally published.

Litigation brought against Digital Equipment Corporation (and its subsequent incarnations) related to these studies was finally settled in 2009. In this action, it was claimed that the company had failed to supply a safe system of work for those employed within the 'clean rooms' developed to manufacture its semiconductors. The production processes employed by Digital had allowed dermal exposure to harmful chemicals, and in so doing, had caused long-term harm to employees, birth defects among their offspring and spontaneous foetal abortion. None of this was known to Peters and Waterman (1982), although given the selective deafness and blindness of the authors we have to wonder whether this issue – had it been known more generally in the late 1970s – would have featured within their analysis of business excellence. What is clear, however, is that the issues arising around dermal exposure to ethylene glycol esters *should* have been known to Schein (2003) and would have been known to Olsen. But we hear nothing on this matter. Indeed within a lengthy account of the company's cultural practices and preferences, no question is raised as to the extent to which Digital's values might have been tested by evidence that its production processes had been known to cause harm to employees since 1982; the date of the first publication of *In Search of Excellence.*

Of course critics may choose to point out that that Digital's failure to supply a safe system of work for those engaged in the manufacture of semiconductors does little to explain its demise. And in this they may be correct. Nonetheless it is worth pointing out that while Digital's failure to safeguard the health of its employees (and the health of their unborn children) may have had little bearing upon the company's ultimate decline, it should have a bearing upon the manner in which we consider and account for its success.

As we close this case report it may be useful to observe that Simpson (2017) offers an alarming postscript to our re-view of *Delta's* legacy. He observes that from 1995, the high-technology industry in the US has managed the inherent toxicity of its production processes through a time-honoured expedient. It has exported the production of semiconductors to South Korea, which in having, we must assume, prominent business genes within its DNA has made its entrepreneurial *untermenschen* available for our convenience. Suffer the little children indeed!

Emerson Electrical

Emerson was established in 1890 in St. Louis, Missouri to manufacture the electric motors earlier patented by the Metson brothers. Two years later the company expanded its product range to offer electric fans and soon thereafter began to produce sewing machines as well as a variety of power tools and dental drills. During World War II the company became the largest manufacturer of armaments for military aircraft.

In the postwar period the company was led by WR Buck who served as president from 1954 to 1973. During this period the company acquired 36 companies. On the eve of Buck's retirement, Emerson had 82 plants, 31,000 employees and had recently posted sales worth $800 million. WR Buck was succeeded by Chuck Knight in 1973. Knight, like his predecessor, served as president for 19 years and continued the diversification strategy previously adopted by Buck. It is worth observing that where Buck chose to acquire just 36 companies during his time in office, Knight secured the acquisition of more than 200 companies during his time at the helm.

Knight has produced an extensive account of his leadership practice and philosophy (Knight with Dyer, 2005). This text is interesting at a number of levels. It demonstrates for example the manner in which the precepts of *In Search of Excellence* (Peters and Waterman, 1982); the need to demonstrate 'a bias for action', the need to secure 'productivity through people,' and the virtues of being 'close to the customer' have become central to the discourse of business practice. In addition, Knight's reflections on his own leadership practices offers illuminating insights on Emerson's core values and the limitations of this espoused philosophy. Indeed it is worth observing that Emerson's strategy of growth by acquisition, while successful in narrow financial terms (see Knight with Dyer, 2005: x–xi) demonstrates that the company did not, in fact, subscribe to the full package of behavioural attributes said to be necessary for business excellence and most certainly *did not* 'stick to the knitting'!

Reflecting upon his personal philosophy of management, Knight (Knight with Dyer, 2005: 4) insists that Emerson's management process contains 'six key elements that boil down to a simple formula.' This formula, he tells us, rests on a 'foundation of core beliefs that are mutually consistent and reinforcing' (4). These mutually consistent and reinforcing values we are advised reflect a concern with 'integrity' and 'shared commitment' (4). All employees we are assured 'want the same thing: consistent and high performance' (5). This (unsubstantiated claim) allows Knight to insist that profitability is both, a state of mind and an outcome that is secured when autonomy is granted to those managers who are close to the customer. In this regard Knight's espoused philosophy plainly embraces the central precepts of excellence as outlined by Peters and Waterman (1982). Thus, Knight advises that managerial leaders need to be committed to success, need to concentrate on positives and possibilities and must develop and maintain a strong sense of urgency (Knight with Dyer, 2005: 10). And yet, Knight is clear that beyond target-setting and people management, managerial work within Emerson turns upon 'identifying and successfully implementing business investment opportunities that support the company's targets for growth and profitability' (6). And there's the rub! Thus it is clear that despite Knight's focus upon values and integrity, and despite his assertion that his is a people-driven organization, (populated by good folks who all want the same thing), Emerson remains a conglomerate organization that is perfectly willing to divest itself of those *units* deemed to be under-performing. Between 1983 and 1988, for example, Emerson closed 50 plants in the US while simultaneously expanding production in low-wage countries. The fate of those cast from what we are assured is the happy collective that is Emerson does not detain Knight and in truth does not feature in his philosophy of management. We must assume therefore that these employees – employees we must assume who continued to want the very same things as Knight even as they were shown the door – are, truthfully, of little lingering consequence. The fate of those employees who may have felt the need to probe Knight's philosophy and who, in so doing, sought collective representation has, however, been documented, albeit not by Knight. That said, and in all fairness, we should concede that Knight does offer some insight on his posture towards organized labour. *Emerson's* philosophy is he tells us 'communicative' and not 'participative.' What others might classify as a participative form of management, built upon and mediated by trade union organization is, Knight insists 'unnecessary if management does its job well' (Knight with Dyer, 2005: 57).

But what might it mean to do your job well in this context?

Knight's response resolves to a communication plan instituted in 1954 as a response, we should note, to collective action within the Emerson business empire. Yet, court papers produced in the context of Emerson Electric Company versus National Labor Relations Board demonstrate the nature of this 'communicative' approach to management and the lengths that the company is prepared to go to in order to oppose union organizations.

The case brought by Emerson arose as a consequence of an organizing campaign conducted by Local 574 of the Teamsters union at Emerson's Kennett plant. The union did not succeed in this campaign. It lost the recognition vote cast on November 1975. Suspecting management interference in the recognition process, however, the union sought a legal remedy. The court agreed and found for the union. However, Emerson chose to appeal. On April 6, 1978 the appellant court again found for the union. The court confirmed that Emerson had conducted a campaign of surveillance against its employees. It had taken steps to reduce meaningful discussion of union matters. It had also threatened employees with discharge, with plant closure and with loss of benefits. And if all that were not bad enough the company was found to have conducted a campaign of harassment and intimidation against two named individuals.

For those who have any knowledge of US industrial relations this may come as little surprise. What *should be* surprising is that two McKins*ey* partners – two putative business gurus, namely Peters and Waterman (1982) – seem to have been either unaware of these events *or* had knowledge of these events but had decided that this conduct was not inconsistent with a business philosophy built upon people-driven productivity, community and integrity.

Some years ago Tom Peters was forced to address the allegation that he and Bob Waterman had faked the data that they used to justify their formulation of business excellence (see Peters, 2001b). For the record, we have never set much store by this allegation. Peters did not fake his data. Truthfully, he and Bob Waterman had none to fake for as the Bechtel case makes clear and as the Emerson case reveals, the authors simply lacked the insights on company operations and practice necessary to substantiate their core claims. The problem being, of course, that in the absence of any more searching account of the political economy of US business the field of management studies has, for 40 years, a) built its practice upon a prospectus that is inconsistent and woefully incomplete and has b) based its prescriptions upon an account of the ways and means of management that is, as the courts have shown, often detrimental to good governance.

Fluor

Fluor Corporation has its origins in a saw and paper mill, partnership formed between the three Fluor brothers in 1890. The company expanded from milling to become the Fluor Brothers Construction Company in 1903 and prospered in this period by gearing its production expertise to meet the needs of the growing US petroleum industry. In 1924, the company was incorporated and in 1957 offered its shares to the public for the first time.

Today the company is one of the largest engineering and construction businesses in the world although to describe the company in these terms would be to disguise the reach of its operations. Thus, beyond construction and engineering the company's activities include renting, selling and servicing construction equipment; consultancy work; and a variety of human resources services.

Fluor has worked closely with Saudi Arabia's ARAMCO since the 1940s, building oil refineries amongst other projects. Later the company would undertake similar engagements on behalf of Iran and South Korea. Since 1967, Fluor has been actively involved in the off-shore drilling industry and has, thanks to the acquisition of related companies, been actively involved in mining since 1969. The corporation also has considerable investments in the coal industry, and holds these in collaboration with a consortium, which includes Bechtel. In common with Caterpillar, Fluor chose to establish production facilities with South Africa's racist, apartheid regime although it divested this holding in 1986 . . . for business reasons.

During the early 1970s the company grew at an extraordinary rate. In 1973, it posted earnings of $1.3 billion which rose to $4.4 billion in 1974 and some $9 billion in 1975. In recent years Fluor, has extended its production expertise and has, like Bechtel, secured very large projects associated with the nuclear power industry. And, again in common with Bechtel, Fluor has also attracted controversy relating to its business partners and indeed its broader dealings.

In the mid-1970s the Kingdom of Saudi Arabia approached its key business partners with a funding proposition designed to advance the standing and reputation of the territory. The Kingdom sought funding of some $20 million for this endeavour and offered the reassurance that donations were required to avoid the charge that it was simply involved in a blatant propaganda exercise. Fluor contributed $1 million to this 'soft power' project. However, controversy arose around the formation of a Middle East Studies Centre at the University of Southern California made possible by these donations.

It was alleged that the University's Board of Trustees, which was at this time chaired by Fluor's chief executive, had sought to attach conditions to the funding of the Middle East Studies Centre that were not only inappropriate infringements of academic freedom but anti-Israeli in orientation and, indeed, reflective of a deeper anti-Semitism. *The New York Times* in a series of articles (see 11/02/1979; 28/08/1979; 11/09/1979) charts this developing controversy and the company's response. The newspaper (11/02/1979) notes for example the resignation of Dr. Hubbard, President of the University of Southern California against the backdrop of claims that those charged with the oversight of the endowment had sought to exercise improper influence on the University (*The New York Times* 28/08/1979). The newspaper also reports that Jewish leaders, the student body and members of the faculty had all voiced concerns over the establishment of the centre and its anti-Semitic orientation. *The New York Times* (28/08/1979 also allowed Fluor a right of response. Quoting Mr Etter, then the Vice President for Public Relations at Fluor, the newspaper reported the company's position. Mr. Etter reassured readers the charges of anti-Semitism were bogus confections: 'This whole affair,' he advised 'has been distorted by the Jewish press.'

And who could possibly take issue with that sort of hands-on; value-driven management?

Weitz and Luxenberg attorneys[13] would and have. Citing a judgement passed down in February 2016, the law firm advises that they have secured damages in excess of $5million for a client, whom a jury decided had been harmed by the reckless conduct of those stewarding two subsidiaries of the

Fluor corporation. This judgment concerns the manner in which Fluor had managed fabrication processes involving the use of asbestos, the highly toxic, carcinogen which we encountered when discussing Dana.

Readers may protest of course that this court judgement post-dates the birth of the excellence project by almost 40 years. And that observation is perfectly correct. But it overlooks one key fact: the carcinogenic effects of asbestos take some time to reveal themselves. Thus, while it is true that the court's decision was handed down many years after the publication of *In Search of Excellence*, the substance of the case won by *Weitz and Luxenberg* relates to the activities of Fluor and two of its subsidiaries during the 1950s, 1960s and the 1970s when the company was being lauded by Peters and Waterman (1982). In court it was established that the plaintiff had contracted cancer due to exposure to asbestos. Noting that the company's attitude to this risk had been reckless, the jury chose to award punitive damages. Doubtless the decision as to the level of damages awarded was influenced by the revelation that the corporation had continued to use asbestos in Iran, exposing the plaintiff to continuing harm, even after it its use on US soil had been prohibited!

Fluor merits just five mentions within *In Search of Excellence*. Two of these entries amount to an endorsement of the corporation's focus and strategic orientation. Fluor, we are assured is, like Bechtel, a star in the field of project management and has achieved its star status by 'sticking to the knitting.' Two more entries praise the company for having 'a bias for action' with the final entry is reserved for an endorsement of its 'lean' staffing policy: the company we are told runs 'its $6 billion operations with three corporate planners' (Peters and Waterman, 1982: 312). No mention is made of the remaining attributes said to be necessary for the achievement of business excellence. We hear nothing of 'customers,' for example, and you would search in vain for any sustained account of culture and/ or values. And that is probably just as well because any sustained reflection on the corporation's policies and orientations might have revealed to Peters and Waterman that which had become clear to the *New York Times*, namely that Fluor was profoundly anti-Semitic, had questionable friends, few policies dedicated to the provision of safe working conditions and fewer scruples when it came to serving the needs of its clientele.

Hewlett Packard (HP)

Bill Hewlett and Dave Packard met at Stanford University (not Stamford as Gibbs (2020) suggests in his self-published account!) in the 1930s when they were both students. They formed Hewlett Packard in a garage in 1939, choosing the company name it is claimed, on the toss of a coin (see Packard,

1995). Readers (schooled in the axiomatic belief that all successful organizations proceed on the basis of a detailed plan that must then be very carefully implemented) may be alarmed to learn that as Hewlett and Packard embarked upon their joint business venture they had no clear plan or business model. Despite this (although some would protest that it might be more helpful to begin this sentence with the words 'because of this') the company was successful through the war years and was incorporated in 1947. A decade later it offered shares to the public.

In the early days of its existence the company had accepted contracts on work such as auto-flush urinals and (mild) electric shock devices conceived as aids to weight loss. What might be called Hewlett Packard's first product, which built squarely upon the engineering expertise of its founders was an audio-oscillator machine that it sold to Disney.

In the mid-1960s the company began to expand its product range to include the electronic devices for which it is now chiefly known. During this period, for example, Hewlett Packard pioneered the desk-top, electronic calculator and in 1972 produced the first truly pocket calculator. In 1966 the company produced its first computer, the 2116A, and in 1972 it launched its own mini-computer as a rival to the mainframe computers offered by such stalwarts as IBM. However, the 1970s and 1980s, it supplemented what had been until this point a relatively low volume, high margin business model with a range of products – desk-top personal computers and printers – which were produced in high volume for a low profit margin. To secure returns in this context, the company was obliged to develop innovations in its product design (designing modular power units that would allow it to produce printers for a range of different territories within a single production facility) and its manufacturing process (being, for example, a pioneer of *kanban* production in the US).

Hewlett Packard was, from its inception, guided by a set of core principles that reflect the ideals of its founders. Recognizing the centrality of these ideas, the founders chose to formalize the company's core values when it became publicly quoted in 1957. In 1966, the company reviewed and refined these values. In his account of The HP Way, Packard (1995) renders these as follows:

1   Profitability is the single best measure of the company's contribution to society and the ultimate source of its corporate strength and vitality. The company should, therefore, produce the maximum level of profit that is consistent with its core objectives.
2   Customers seek and may expect continual improvements in the products available. To this end the company should focus upon 'quality, usefulness and value' (Packard, 1995: 81) in its products and services.

3   The company should understand its core field of interest and should limit its endeavours to this field. Or more plainly, Packard (1995) argued that the company should 'stick to the knitting.'

4   Company growth is a measure of strength and is, furthermore, a pre-requisite for survival.

5   Employees must share in the success of the company and should enjoy satisfying work that provides a sense of accomplishment. In addition, workers should enjoy job security based upon their performance.

6   The organization should foster initiative and creativity and should provide employees with the latitude necessary to pursue established objectives. To enable this Hewlett Packard employed certain key innovations – 'management by objectives,' 'management by wandering around,' and 'open-door' management – that have since become central to the excellence project and to the day-to-day practice of contemporary management.

7   The organization has an obligation to contribute to the community and to the institutions which generate the company's larger operating context. In other words, the company should consider itself to be a citizen and should conduct itself accordingly.

Yet while such words are easy to mouth there are good reasons to believe that they were not simply 'boiler-plate.' The founders, for example, both retained life-long commitments to philanthropy and in their day-to-day practice were clear that the leadership ideals they had formalized would need to be fostered by a hands-on approach to management that has become immortalized as MBWA or 'management by wandering around.' Doubtless it was a combination of these practices and values and, of course, the company's success as an innovator within a market at the leading edge of technological development that caused Peters and Waterman (1982) to celebrate Hewlett Packard as an exemplar of excellence. Yet, while the company has been presented as a distinctive, visionary, values-led organization it might be more accurate to suggest that Hewlett Packard had simply honoured and maintained a set of practices which other large organizations, born in an earlier era such as Cadbury, Lever Brothers and Colman had understood to be, both, proper and productive! And while there is no evidence to suggest that Hewlett Packard stooped to the corrupt practices of Bechtel and Boeing, it is worth observing that the public articulation (and celebration) of such practical values did not prevent Hewlett Packard from opening a production facility in Johannesburg, South Africa in 1980 even as this country continued to practice the racist policy of segregation known as 'apartheid.'

IBM

The International Business Machines Corporation was formed in 1924 when Thomas Watson gained control of C-T-R (The Computing-Tabulating-Recording Company) from his employer CR Flint (DeLamarter [1986] 1988: 11). Watson had joined Flint's 'industrial consolidation' (DeLamarter [1986] 1988: 11) in 1914 having been dismissed by NCR, which was at this time a manufacturer of cash registers. Watson's dismissal arose as a consequence of events which had begun to unfold two years earlier. In February 1912 Watson and a number of other executives employed by NCR became the first people to be charged under 'anti-trust' legislation in the US. The defendants endured a three-month trial and 'were declared guilty of criminal conspiracy in restraint of trade and of maintaining a monopoly' (DeLamarter, [1986] 1988: 10). Each received the maximum sentence available to the court; a one year jail term and a $5,000 fine but were released under bail conditions pending an appeal hearing.

Following his conviction Watson was dismissed by Patterson, the boss of NCR. It may be useful to note, however, that DeLamarter ([1986] 1988: 10–11) refuses to absolve Patterson. Indeed he characterizes Patterson as a dominating, if paranoid presence who had, in fact, instructed Watson in the dark arts of anti-competitive practice. Watson never did serve his sentence: a retrial was ordered on a procedural technicality but the case against Watson and his co-defendants was not placed before the courts again.

The key product offered by Watson's new employer, C-T-R was the tabulating machine developed by the German engineer, Hollerith. Black (2001) characterizes Flint, the owner and controller of C-T-R as a war-profiteer who built his business on contracts with the US Census Bureau. Flint's business model, De Lamarter suggests set the pattern for the practices that Watson would later employ within IBM: he chose to lease the Hollerith tabulating machines to customers, deriving much of his income from the sale of consumables. Commenting upon this business practice, DeLamarter ([1986] 1988: 14) notes that by the end of the war, C-T-R was 'selling blank [punch] cards at the rate of more than 80 million a month.'

In the 1930s Watson became the highest paid executive in the US thanks to an arrangement which granted a salary plus 5% of company profits. Black (2001) asserts that during this period IBM worked closely with Germany's Nazi regime through a German subsidiary (acquired in 1922). Furthermore Black (2001) alleges that IBM maintained these business arrangements with the Nazis throughout World War II. Indeed he insists that IBM designed the very instruments that enabled expropriation and, ultimately genocide.

In the US and Britain IBM was we should acknowledge (also) a key contributor to the allied war effort. Black (2001) reminds us that IBM had set itself up to provide business solutions for customers and indeed continues to pride itself on its ability to anticipate and in so doing to shape customer requirements. He notes that in the aftermath of the Japanese attack on Pearl Harbour, IBM predicted that the US government would soon require data that would allow it to identify and, subsequently, to intern resident foreign nationals such that when the State Department sought to initiate discussions around this project, IBM personnel were already on the job!

Highlighting IBM's contribution to the allied war effort, Black (2001) reminds us that the company provided punch card readers, collaters and alphabetizers; pre-cursors to the modern digital computer, which allowed the military to plan and to manage the day-to-day conduct of the war as well as larger strategic endeavours including the planning efforts required for the allied landings in Normandy; the analysis of the effectiveness of the US bombing campaign over Japan; and the code-breaking efforts of those working at Bletchley Park. Beyond this it is perhaps worth noting that IBM production facilities also manufactured weapons for the military including light and heavy machine guns.

Peters and Waterman (1982) invite us to view IBM, which by 1985 had become the most profitable company in the world, delivering some $6.6 billion in profits to its shareholders on revenues in excess of $50 billion (DeLamarter [1986] 1988: xiv–xv) as owing its success to a) its action orientation and b) its willingness to get close to the customer. Indeed given the extent to which Peters and Waterman (1982) focus upon IBM at the expense of other organizations (see Collins, 2022) there is good reason to suggest that IBM represented, for the authors at least, *the* exemplary model of the exemplars of excellence. Yet DeLamarter ([1986] 1988: xviii) argues that this familiar characterization of IBM is, frankly 'dead wrong.' Indeed DeLamarter ([1986] 1988: xviii) insists that IBM's success comes not from its commitment to the organizational attributes of excellence but 'from the power of monopoly' (xviii).

Reflecting upon the extent to which IBM has used its monopoly position to secure market share and excess profits, De Lamarter argues that the company, in the shape of Watson, father and son, have played a cat-and-mouse game with customers and regulators for more than a century. Indeed, De Lamarter notes that Watson's first conviction for a breach of anti-trust regulations in 1912 was followed by further, federal anti-trust proceedings in 1932. The company was found guilty of these charges but chose to appeal this decision all the way to the Supreme Court. In 1936, however, the company was obliged to change its practices when it lost its final appeal. A further case was brought against IBM in 1952 but was dropped by the authorities in 1956 when the company voluntarily agreed to reduce its market share of the punched cards business from 85% to 50% (DeLamarter [1986] 1988: 23). Furthermore we should acknowledge that while Peters and Waterman (1982) were preparing the text of *In Search of Excellence,*

IBM was, in fact, fighting 'dozens of private anti-trust cases' (DeLamarter [1986] 1988: xiv) filed concurrently *and* a further case brought by the Attorney General in charge of the Anti-trust Division.

Challenging the representation of IBM that is preferred by Peters and Waterman (1982); a depiction we should note, which makes no mention of the company's various convictions and compromise deals, DeLamarter ([1986] 1988: xviii) offers an alternative rationalization for the company's growth and success. IBM's success, he warns (DeLamarter [1986] 1988: xviii) is not the result of 'the healthy interplay of competitive forces' *and does not* derive from its adherence to the eight attributes of excellence. Thumbing his nose at the core claims of the excellence project, DeLamarter ([1986] 1988: xvi) insists that:

> IBM is at times poorly managed, its products inferior, its customers unhappy and its actions ruthless if not illegal.

Johnson & Johnson

Johnson & Johnson was founded by three brothers, Robert, James and Edward Johnson, in 1886 to produce surgical dressings designed to reduce, what was in a pre-antibiotic era, the very real risk of post-operative infection. The company was incorporated in 1887 and has, since this date, worked to improve the efficacy of its surgical dressings. In 1893 the company launched its famous baby powder and in 1921 introduced the familiar self-adhesive dressing that is marketed as Band-Aid.

In 1919 Johnson & Johnson chose to expand their operations beyond the US, moving into Canada prior to opening a subsidiary in England. Thanks to the acquisition of the McNeil Laboratories in 1959 the company was able to secure the rights to Tylenol, an over-the-counter pain medication. It is worth noting however that this product only achieved true, mass-market penetration in 1975 when Johnson & Johnson reduced the retail price in order to counter the competition posed by the suppliers of similar, generic pain-killers.

Robert Johnson became company President in 1932 and developed the divisionalization strategy, much admired by Peters and Waterman (1982: 272, 309, 310). Between 1932 and 1968 (the year of Robert Johnson's death) company sales rose from $11 million to $700 million, partly due to the company's decision to extend its product line from healthcare into more general consumer products such as sanitary napkins. By 1978 thanks, in part, to the efforts of those brand and marketing specialists recruited from Procter and Gamble, Johnson & Johnson had secured 50% of the market for 'feminine hygiene products. While such sales growth is undoubtedly impressive the company is perhaps more commonly recognized for the 'credo,' which Robert Johnson penned in 1943 just before the company's stock became publicly quoted.

Today, the Johnson & Johnson credo spells out the company's core responsibilities to an extended collection of stakeholders. Primary among these stakeholders, we are assured are the patients, doctors nurses (and beyond these groups the mothers and fathers of all those) who use the company's products. The company is dedicated to providing value, through reduced costs and reasonably priced products.

The company's second responsibility is to its employees. These employees we are told deserve a working environment that is inclusive; which respects diversity; which offers workers dignity and respect, and which demonstrates ethical choices in and through its leadership.

The third responsibility of the company is to the communities which host its production facilities. Johnson & Johnson we are told has an obligation to act as a good corporate citizen, supporting community health and education initiatives through charitable donation and by shouldering its fair share of the tax burden. The company's fourth responsibility – and this ordering is crucial – is to its stockholders. Johnson & Johnson is obliged to engage in research and development activities and is, furthermore, obliged to invest in innovative technologies and processes, while maintaining reserves that will enable a fair return to shareholders in good times and under less advantageous conditions.

This 'credo,' which pre-dates the 'HP Way,' by some 14 years has become a touchstone for the company and for business commentators. Indeed Johnson & Johnson has been celebrated for this four-fold declaration of values.

In 1982 the credo was publicly tested when seven people died due to the consumption of Tylenol, which had been deliberately contaminated with potassium cyanide. Responding to this crisis, Johnson and Johnson chose to clear the shelves of its products to avoid further harm to its primary stakeholders. The suppliers of the generic alternative to Tylenol experienced a bonanza in the aftermath of this decision while 18% was wiped from the value of Johnson & Johnson stock. Nonetheless the company continued to communicate openly with the press and issued coupons to compensate those consumers who had chosen to dispose of their existing stocks of Tylenol. When the authorities issued new guidelines on packaging security designed to limit any future attempts to adulterate products, Johnson & Johnson led the way with a three-layered approach to protective packaging.

Thanks to the company's efforts sales of Tylenol had returned to 90% of pre-1982 levels by 1989. James Burke, who served as company Chief Executive Officer between 1976 and 1989 received plaudits for his management of this crisis and was inducted into the Business Hall of Fame in 1990. In recent years however the extent to which the company truly honours its credo has been called into question. Indeed the *Guardian* newspaper (18/10/2019) has suggested that, today, Johnson & Johnson faces an existential threat. This threat arises, in part, due to the discovery of asbestos in the company's baby talcum powder. This is a concern, we should note, that has been discussed publicly since at least 1976 when independent researchers published the results of their inquiries into the contents of commercially available powders. The researchers sampled 15 talcum powders marketed by some of the leading suppliers and reported contamination levels ranging from 2 to 20% in 10 of the products (*New York Times*, 10/03/1976). None of the products offered by Johnson & Johnson were reported as being contaminated. The company therefore continued to offer its baby powder to the public and as late as 2019 continued to insist that a product recall of its talcum powder was in no way associated with concerns related to asbestos contamination (*New York Times*, 29/10/2019). Yet, this public reassurance was offered despite the fact that earlier reports had revealed a) the company's awareness of this issue and b) its failure to over-turn a verdict which had awarded $4.7 billion in punitive damages to a plaintiff who had contracted ovarian cancer through use of the company's products (*New York Times*, 15/ 12/2018; 20/12/2018).

Commenting upon the broader picture and on the company's prospects, the *Guardian* (18/10/2019) has suggested Johnson & Johnson now faces liabilities in the region of $15 billion despite having settled some 14,000 cases related to ovarian cancer. Highlighting the source of these cancers the newspaper reveals that between 1972 and 1975 three separate laboratories had tested the company's talcum powders and had found these to be contaminated, often, with high levels of asbestos. Yet – and despite its credo – the company chose to keep this knowledge from the US Food and Drugs Administration (FDA).

It would be wrong of course to suggest that Peters and Waterman (1982) had any knowledge of this terrible scandal as they prepared their account of business excellence. Truthfully they appear to have been duped just like the rest of us. Given this sorry state of affairs we choose to conclude with two (admittedly) rhetorical questions:

> Is it necessary to rehearse the ways in which the company's shameful conduct during the 1970s – and since that date – runs prior to its own credo and to the core attributes of excellence?
> Would it be churlish to ask if the image of James Burke (CEO between 1976 and 1989) still graces the Business Hall of Fame?

McDonald's

Love (1986) offers a very engaging account of McDonald's origins and development. Yet there are at least three factors beyond the lucidity of its prose that make this text interesting and useful for our purposes. Firstly,

Love's (1986: 8) analysis demonstrates that a mere four years after the publication of *In Search of Excellence*, the core concerns and orientations of Peters and Waterman (1982) had already become a part of the day-to-discourse of management:

> At a time when American corporations are looking to emulate their foreign rivals the story of McDonald's reminds us that business can still succeed – beyond their creator's wildest dreams – by relying on typically American traits.
>
> (Love, 1986: 8)

Indeed the fact that Love finds it unnecessary to elaborate upon the 'typically American traits' that are said to underpin McDonald's success serves only to demonstrate the extent to which calls to a core and essential Americanism had gone beyond being simply, something that was commonly voiced to become instead, something natural and obvious; something that since it required no further explanation or elaboration could be accepted tacitly.

Secondly Love's (1986: 8 emphasis in original) text suggests that, despite the focus which Peters and Waterman had placed upon IBM, there is good reason to suggest that it is, in truth, McDonald's that might be taken to be the very archetype of business excellence:

> The history of the McDonald's system is the story of an organization that learned how to harness the power of entrepreneurs – not several but hundreds of them. It is run by decisions and policies considered to be for the common good. But the definition of *common good* is not set by a chief executive or by a management committee. Rather, it is the product of the interaction between all the players. Ray Kroc's genius was building a system that requires all of its members to follow corporate-like rules but at the same time rewards them for expressing their individual creativity. In essence the history of McDonald's is a case study on managing entrepreneurs in a corporate setting.

Thirdly Love (1986) offers an account of McDonald's, which while it shares the celebratory, managerialist[14] tone of the analysis developed by Peters and Waterman (1982), does at least extend this account to offer a more fully developed historical analysis of the company. Notably this account, in taking us beyond the executive suite confirms the success of *McDonald's* while tracing the manner in which the company has, truthfully, developed systems of management that have revolutionized the industry. In this respect Love allows us to understand why it is that 'McDonalidization' has, like 'Taylorism' and 'Fordism' become a shorthand expression designed to express and to explore our experience of modern organizations.

Love's (1986: 30) account of McDonald's success gives a starring role to Ray Kroc, the former cup salesman who was, by 1954, the representative of a company making kitchen equipment for commercial catering organizations. Kroc, he reminds us, did not found McDonald's. This honour goes to two brothers – McDonalds by birth – who opened a small, drive-in diner in Pasadena, California in 1937. This diner we should note was, despite its small scale, both popular and profitable. Indeed Love (1986) reports that by the mid-1940s the diner was posting annual sales of $200,000 and was generating profits in the region of $100,000. By 1948, however, the brothers, while comfortably well-off, had become bored by the day-to-day challenges which this business posed. Highlighting these challenges, Love suggests that the brothers were subject to competition for customers and for staff. Consequently he tells us McDonald's faced wage pressures and larger managerial issues caused by staff turnover and by rising costs. It seems that initially the partners made plans to sell their drive-in business and considered buying a more conventional restaurant before choosing an altogether more radical strategy. This strategic change, familiar now but radical at the time, led the brothers to simplify their menu (they had come to understand that 80% of their business flowed from just one line on their menu – hamburgers) and to sack their 'carhops' (or waiting staff) in favour of a self-service approach.

Initially the partners struggled to convince their clientele of the merits of their new approach and indeed many of their traditional patrons – the teenagers who preferred to drive up and hang out – simply moved on to other outlets which retained the services of carhops. Yet, Love suggests that the loss of this traditional clientele transformed McDonald's from a somewhat dangerous and liminal zone (where the conventional norms governing social relations were, let's say relaxed) to become instead a family-friendly place, where parents and children would choose to come to eat. Within six months, (thanks in part to changes within the kitchen area which saw the introduction of specially designed equipment and the advent of a detailed division of labour that sub-divided cooking and food preparation tasks), the business had returned to the performance levels, which had been attained prior to the shutdown necessary to effect the redesign. Indeed by 1951 the new diner was posting sales of $277,000, which rose to some $350,000 by 1955 (Love, 1986: 19).

This growing business brought some level of notoriety to their operations and by 1952, when it seemed to the brothers that they were spending much of each working week explaining their business model they decided that they should consider franchising the company. The approach to franchising that was developed by the brothers McDonald, however, was pretty rudimentary. In effect, the brothers sold their name and simply allowed their franchisees to get on with it. It was Ray Kroc; Love's (1986: 30) 'genius,' who understood the limits of this approach and who in seeking a remedy, effectively developed the larger organizational apparatus that we now know as McDonald's.

Kroc, who had first encountered McDonald's in 1954 and who soon after took a primary role in the development and management of its franchise operations, had, by 1957 (Love, 1986: 151) established the successful formula that has allowed the company to offer a consistently high standard of quality and service across its estate. Yet a problem remained. Everyone within the extended chain of connections that, in effect, constituted McDonald's – the founders; the franchisees and the suppliers – was making money. But the company itself regularly struggled to cover its own payroll costs (Love, 1986: 176). Recognizing this problem, Harry Sonneborn suggested a further innovation that 'converted McDonald's into a money machine' (Love, 1986: 152). In effect Sonneborn argued that the company should form a real estate subsidiary, with a view to buying property that it would then lease to its franchisees at a margin. This development transformed the fortunes of the company. It allowed *McDonald's* company to acquire a real estate portfolio and, crucially from Kroc's perspective, provided a lever that would allow *McDonald's* to ensure that its franchisees would be obliged to conform, fully, to the company's expectations as regards service and quality standards. Building upon this understanding of the company's operating principles Love (1986: 323) suggests that it would be a mistake to suggest that *McDonald's* is involved in the fast-food service business. Instead he insists that the company is more properly viewed as a leader in the food processing and distribution business and has developed an extended and integrated value chain to assure its operation. Highlighting the extent of this business, Love (1986: 2) reminds us that by the mid-1980s the company had come to dominate America's $130 billion food service industry (which was at the time roughly double the size of the domestic computer industry). Indeed he observes that by the mid-1980s, the company, alone, consumed 7.5% of the country's potato harvest. Furthermore he reminds us that *McDonald's* had become a major player in the advertising arena by virtue of the fact that, by the mid-1980s, it was spending around $600 million on promotional activity each year (Love, 1986: 1).

Commenting upon the company's track-record of innovation, Love returns to the entrepreneurial themes that frame his introductory remarks to point out that *McDonald's* owes much of its success to innovations developed beyond the immediate environs of the company. Key additions to the company's menus, he observes were in fact developed by individual franchisees, whereas the move from a fresh to frozen food supply chains was, in fact, led by its suppliers in the face of the company's skepticism. Yet while acknowledging all of this, Love is keen to remind us that Kroc's 'genius' was to notice and allow such innovation. Indeed, he argues that thanks to Kroc's energy and commitment *McDonald's* has been able to scale local menu changes across its network and, often, years before its rivals.

In recent decades the company has often been attacked by a broad base of critics. Some have suggested for example that its products and its business operations are damaging to the environment while others have argued that *McDonald's* promotes unhealthy eating among children and adults and is, consequently a contributor to the obesity crisis. Others meanwhile have suggested that *McDonald's* is at the forefront of a project of Americanization that is damaging to local cultures. And some have used the company's own core branding technique to highlight the creeping development of 'McJobs'; low-skilled, low-status and low-paid forms of employment that offer no meaningful long-term prospects for advance. Peters and Waterman (1982) were however very much enamoured of *McDonald's* and in their account of business excellence chose to highlight the company's growth and its networked innovation. Consequently they offer no meaningful critical commentary on the organization. Of course it would be completely wrong to castigate Peters and Waterman for their failure to address concerns and criticisms that have arisen subsequent to the publication of their text. The concept of the 'McJob' is after all a recent development and the environmental concerns that *McDonald's* has sought to address in recent years were, frankly, fairly marginal concerns as the authors toiled to produce *In Search of Excellence* in the late 1970s. Nonetheless there *were* critical perspectives voiced against *McDonald's* in this period that Peters and Waterman (1982) should have understood but simply failed to address. Love (1986: 360–361) notes for example that the company was castigated for making campaign contributions to Nixon's election campaign and was accused of using these payments to secure an amendment to legislation on the minimum wage (the exemption of students) that would greatly benefit *McDonald's*. Love, of course, suggests that there is no evidence to support this claim and protests that the company never invoked this exemption. But scandal there was!

Love (1986: 361) also reminds us that the company courted controversy and was, again, accused of exercising political influence when it successfully persuaded those charged with the statutory management of prices and incomes that it should be allowed to raise the price of its quarter-pounder by 4 cents. Beyond these party political concerns, Love observes that the company became embroiled in the civil rights protest and was subject to a boycott in Cleveland, Ohio when it became apparent that it had no African-American franchisees (see *The New York Times* 16/07/1969; 25/01/1970; *Business Week*, 17/12/2021). Love (1986: 362) points out that this state of affairs arose, innocently enough. *McDonald's* restricted the proportion of cash that franchisees could borrow to launch their business and larger structural inequalities in US society meant that few African-Americans possessed the level of start-up capital necessary. Nonetheless the company did become actively and constructively involved in this protest and subsequently lobbied to improve access to funding for minorities. It is worth noting however that the company withdrew from its engagement with the Cleveland protestors when it became apparent that the Black Panthers were planning, in Love's (1986: 362) words 'a shakedown.'

Meanwhile those who had successfully secured franchises were seeking court judgements on the extent to which *McDonald's* could truly direct their operations. The courts, we should concede, did eventually agree that, in large measure the company could direct the affairs of its franchisees. Yet the point remains – the *McDonald's* business model was being dragged through the courts even as Peters and Waterman were celebrating the company's performance and ethos. Indeed we would do well to note that around this time company became involved in an additional controversy concerning its actual performance (and its credit-worthiness) when its accountants, *Arthur Young*, obliged it to remove $17.4 million of assets from its books (Love, 1986: 174).

Love insists, of course, that many of these scandals were confected. Furthermore he is keen to remind us that the accounting practices, rejected by *Arthur Young*, are now common practice. This may be a fair point yet the larger issue remains: *In Search of Excellence* simply fails to address any of these concerns. And in their celebration of *McDonald's* Peters and Waterman simply fail to explain why those charged with the leadership of the company had, by the mid-1970s, adopted a bunker mentality and had taken the strategic decision not to communicate with the representatives of the print and broadcast media!

Procter and Gamble

Swasy (1993: xiii) begins her account of *Procter and Gamble* with the following observation:

> 'Around the globe Procter and Gamble Co. products take consumers from cradle to grave. Pampers diapers cover babies' bottoms and Ivory soap floats in their bathtubs. Crest toothpaste brushes their teeth and Tide detergent washes their clothes. Folgers coffee starts the workday: Duncan Hines cakes mark each birthday.'

You may protest of course that you use none of these products. You may prefer Luvs to Pampers; Lifeguard to Ivory; Gleem to Crest; Dash to Tide; Tender Leaf to Folgers Coffee; and you may prefer Pringles to sweet cakes and shop accordingly. Yet in this context your preferences make little difference to the outcome for thanks to the competing brand strategy pioneered by *Procter and Gamble* you are, whether or not you realize it, a consumer of the company's wares albeit one that is the subject of careful market testing and complex market segmentation tactics.

Acknowledging the extent to which our kitchen cabinets and bathrooms shelves are occupied by *Procter and Gamble* products, Swasy (1993: 343–356) offers an appendix which, over some fourteen pages documents the full range of products offered by *Procter and Gamble*. This appendix we should note also testifies as to the global reach of the company. Yet having documented the company's full product range, Swasy (1993: 35) offers a more succinct response to the question: what does *Procter and Gamble* make? *Procter and Gamble*, she tells us 'makes the numbers.' It is, in short, and above all else, a company driven by the metrics of quarterly reporting. It is, furthermore a company that seeks 'success at any price' (43) and in its relentless pursuit of success manages its employees by 'fear and intimidation' (43).

Profiling Mr. Artzt who rose from the lowly ranks of 'brand manager' to become the company's CEO in 1989, Swasy (1993: 42–47) paints a picture of a work-obsessed, brash, overly-competitive, output-oriented, selfish, micro-manager. Little wonder perhaps that within and beyond *Procter and Gamble* Artzt acquired the *nom de guerre:* Prince of Darkness. Of course this description of Artzt is hardly unusual. Others, prominent in the corporate world have acquired similar epithets. Harold Geneen, for example, who managed *ITT* during a very, very successful period in its history is often similarly portrayed as a psychologically mal-adjusted bully-boy who regarded *ITT's* sole product to be 'the numbers' (see Pascale and Athos [1981] 1986; Schoenberg, 1985). Yet while Geneen has been vilified and (type)cast as a key factor contributing to the corporate decline experienced by America throughout the 1970s, *Procter and Gamble* has been celebrated as a leading example of business excellence. How might this be explained?

There are, we suggest, at least two potential, if overlapping explanations for this curious state of affairs. Firstly and prosaically, we suggest that *Procter and Gamble* has been celebrated by Peters and Waterman (1982) because the architects of the excellence project chose to indulge a highly superficial account of the company, which overlooked the manifest failings, which Swasy (1993) suggests were abundantly clear to so many of those working within this organization. Secondly we might suggest that Peters and Waterman (1982) had accepted the founding corporate mythology of *Procter and Gamble* as a simple (and untested) reassurance that the organization they encountered in the late 1970s had remained faithful to the vision of its founders and as such offered a good fit for the attributes of excellence that they had conjured to support their developing manifesto and product.

Commenting upon the formation of *Procter and Gamble*, Swasy (1993) reminds us that the company was formed in 1837 when William Procter, an English protestant and candle maker teamed up with James Gamble, an Irish soap maker who shared William's devotion to Protestantism in order to exploit the possibilities made available by Cincinnati's piggeries and the excess fat produced therein. In common with others (such as Messers Cadbury, Colman and Rowntree for example), the religious devotion of William Procter and James Gamble had a profound impact upon the management of their joint enterprise. In the 1860s for example, when the American civil war caused a huge increase in demand for the soap produced by the company and a consequent extension of the working day, the owners still insisted that their factory should close on Sundays to observe the Sabbath. By 1885 *Procter and Gamble* had chosen to reduce the working week from six days to five-and-a-half, closing on Saturday afternoons to afford employees paid leisure time. And in 1887 the company opened perhaps the earliest and certainly the oldest surviving employee profit-sharing scheme in the US. Such innovations, we should note, were followed in 1915 by the provision of sickness and disability insurance for employees. Indeed in 1923 the company offered employees, protection from the lay-offs that typified, then, manufacturing employment by guaranteeing workers continuity of employment and a minimum of 48 weeks of work per year.

While acknowledging the significance of these policies, Swasy (1993) nonetheless suggests that *Procter and Gamble* is an organization that is controlling, secretive to the point of paranoia and actively hostile to any and all who questions its *modus operandi*. Furthermore she makes it abundantly clear that these bullying policies were active and evident even as the company was applauded as an exemplar of business excellence. For example, she notes (Swasy, 1993: 15) that in 1977 Judge Sarah T Hughes had ordered the company to produce an affirmative action plant for its Dallas plant to correct racist hiring and promotion policies. Indeed she suggests that senior executives in this era were brazen in their racism and seemed comfortable in practices that were, albeit at a lower level of intensity, anti-Semitic. As early as 1976 (when Peters and Waterman were of course about to embark upon their inquiries into 'organizational effectiveness') the National Labor Relations Board had found *Procter and Gamble* guilty of numerous labour violations. Furthermore Swasy (1993: 188–189) notes that the company had by this time already chosen to turn its back on its own historic labour management policies and had begun targeting those plants with labour unions for closure. Worse still the company was targeting not just employee collectives but individuals who had come forward to reveal misconduct within the company; singling out for harassment, dismissal and subsequent blacklisting, for example, those employees who had highlighted the manner in which company funds had been misappropriated to fund prostitution (178). But the company's ire was not reserved for employees alone. Those customers who viewed the regime in El Salvador as a murderous dictatorship and who consequently tried to persuade the company to source its coffee beans from another region, were Swasy (1993: 194) observes, soon targeted by the company as were those shareholders who sought to persuade *Procter and Gamble* to reduce its animal testing.

Reflecting upon the manner in which the company managed the controversy that arose around its *Rely* tampons brand and the suggestion that this product had caused the death of a number of young women due to 'toxic shock syndrome,' Swasy offers a dissenting view. She suggests that while the company is nowadays often given credit for withdrawing this product from sale, the truth is that *Procter and Gamble* continued to market the product aggressively to young women, in part, through the wholesale distribution of free samples, even as suspicions as to the link between the product's use and sudden mortality was becoming clearer. In addition, Swasy suggests that the company used covenants built into its research endowments to block the dissemination of research on this important subject and used its own massive financial power to impede the pursuit of justice for those families whose young women had, in effect, been killed by their use of the *Rely* brand of tampons.

Is this the conduct of a company that stands as a beacon for business practice? Is this an organization that is, in a real and positive sense, exemplary?

A final concrete example might prove helpful in this context: When *Procter and Gamble* polluted a river and in so doing poisoned the communities who live around its banks (see Swasy, 1993: 206–234) was it driven by a core set of values to do the right thing?

Did it get close to its customers, listen to the concerns of stakeholders and make amends?

Hardly. It returned to its standard playbook. It denied the problem. It engaged in obfuscation. It placed activists under surveillance and suborned the justice process. And according to Swasy (1993) it hired goons who assaulted and then raped a key local activist who had caused problems for *Procter and Gamble*. Of course the company denies in the strongest possible terms the charges of assault and rape. Indeed we should acknowledge that the company posted a reward designed to secure the arrest and conviction of the assailants. But two things *are* clear enough:

Firstly the company had actively lobbied the authorities to be allowed to dump toxic waste products into the Fenholloway River. Secondly the company employed this concession fully and in so doing poisoned the water course, killing wildlife and damaging the health of the human residents living nearby.

Surely we have the right to expect that a true exemplar of excellence in management would have chosen another course?

Surely a truly responsible, value-driven, customer-oriented organization would not have lobbied for the right to pour toxic, industrial effluent into a water course. And if a truly responsible, value-driven, customer-oriented organization had caused pollution (by error) it would, we suggest, have acknowledged this issue and in demonstrating a bias for action, would surely have taken all appropriate steps to remedy the problem. Excellence is as excellence does.

3M

The Minnesota Mining and Manufacturing Company was founded in 1902.[15] Although the company has long been known as *3M* it did not formally change its name until its centenary year.

There is we should note a certain comedy to the circumstances of the company's formation. Five parties combined to found the Minnesota Mining and Manufacturing Company to manufacture abrasives and duly purchased a mine to supply corundum, the raw material that would supply the necessary abrasives. Unfortunately, the mine yielded anthracite (in the US anthrosite) which was singularly unsuited to these plans. Undeterred the partners resolved to obtain the necessary raw materials by another route so that they could begin to manufacture sandpaper. In 1905 the company opened its first plant but found itself in a crowded market with a low-grade abrasive. Business was not going according to plan. Somehow E B Ober, a principal investor within the original partnership persuaded L B Ordway (by then a self-made millionaire) to invest $25 thousand in the company; $13 thousand to clear the company's existing debts plus an additional $12 thousand to offer working capital. In 1910 3M opened a second plant and over the next few years Ordway pumped a further $250,000 in to the company's coffers. It may be useful to note that no dividend was paid to shareholders until 1916.

The official company history offers a starring role to William McKnight who joined the company in 1914, serving as President between 1929 and 1949 and as Chairman of the Board between 1949 and 1966.[16] During McKnight's tenure the company grew 20-fold, thanks, it is said, to his focus upon learning and innovation. The 3M sales force is said to have been pivotal to these processes; allowing customer problems to drive product development. Indeed it is said that *3M* entered the taped adhesive market (in 1925) when one of the salesmen observed the difficulties which Ford employees experienced when attempting to mask components during the painting process. Similarly the development of 'wet or dry' sandpaper (in 1921) is said to have arisen in response to user demand for an abrasive that did not simply clog and/ or fill the air with choking dust.

The company's successful engagement with its customers allowed it to float on the New York Stock Exchange in 1946. Today the company continues to supply abrasives within a larger product portfolio that runs to some 50,000 items and which draws upon an annual research and development budget of $1 billion.

Peters and Waterman seem to have been quite entranced by 3M. While Delta Airlines (8), Johnson & Johnson (9), Digital Equipment Corporation (14) and Fluor (5) collectively merit only 36 discrete entries in the index[17] of In Search of Excellence, 3M alone merits 43. Indeed just one of these entries runs to some 12 pages and offers a glowing celebration of 3M's ethos and operations (Peters and Waterman, 1982: 223–234).

Highlighting what we are assured are the very distinctive merits of the company, Peters and Waterman (1982: 185, 223) argue that 3M prospers because its 'salesmen' consider themselves to be problem-solvers who work with their customers to develop new and useful innovations. That said the authors are also keen to remind us that at times the sales team, itself has been the source of innovation. Thus Peters and Waterman (1982: 195) suggest that use (and sales) of *Scotch Tape* (first launched in 1930) only really took off when one of the company's salesmen developed a handy dispenser.

While Peters and Waterman (1982) often have a tendency to reduce business processes to those curiously amorphous things we label 'culture' and 'leadership' their treatment of 3M is distinctive and more useful than their other sketches insofar as it focuses upon the manner in which the company (under McKnight's leadership) was structured to ensure purposeful staff rotation (313); the rapid formation of product teams (127); and highly local forms of action which, at times, seems to have enabled the outright subversion of managerial edicts, for example, to cease work on a particular product innovation (215). Underpinning this flexibility is, Peters and Waterman (1982: 127) tell us, a 'leaky' planning system deigned to ensure budget flexibility, overlapping structures (272) and an official tolerance of mistakes (301–302).

Yet, and despite their prolonged focus upon 3M, Peters and Waterman (1982) are curiously silent on a key event, which when it made the national newspapers in 1975 caused the company to lose three of its key officeholders. Discussing these events Jensen (1975) reminds us that while 3M had become officially aware that the company had been making illegal payments to local, state and national politicians in 1974, it had taken no action. In 1975, however, court officials did choose to act. Detailing the extent of 3M's illegal activities, Jensen notes that the company had, for over a decade, managed a money laundering operation which had sent hundreds of thousands of dollars to Switzerland to pay bogus invoices before quietly repatriating this cash to pay (off) local, state and national politicians. When this activity became public knowledge, Hansen the Chief Financial Officer resigned (in November 1974), while Heltzer, the Chief Executive Officer hung on until February 1975. Meanwhile Cross, former CEO and by then the Chairman of the Board announced his intention to stand down. All three of these individuals (and others besides) we should note accepted the charges put to them and were fined for their conduct under civil actions while criminal charges were being considered. The stockmarket reacted predictably to these events. 3M's stock price fell from $80 in 1973 to $56 in 1974 – a fall of 30%. That said in the five years between 1975 and 1980 3M's revenues doubled even as the company chose to withdraw from the magnetic, audio-cassette tape market in the face of fierce price competition from Japan. There is therefore little doubt that 3M has been an extraordinarily successful organization. And there are grounds to believe that the company was similarly distinctive in its managerial and organizational policies. But is this, in the face of clear evidence of a sustained conspiracy to launder money in order to secure influence in local, state and national politics, sufficient to merit the company's inclusion as an exemplar of excellence?

Only you can answer this question of course. Yet the fact that Peters and Waterman (1982) chose to exclude such widely publicized (and unwholesome) dealings from their analytical frame suggests, surely, that 3M's money-laundering conspiracy should have and now *does* invalidate the company's claim to be, truly, an 'exemplar of excellence'; and a model for 'hands-on; value-driven' management.

Concluding Comments

This chapter has considered *In Search of Excellence* at its strongest point. We have not discussed those organizations said to be mostly excellent or only marginally associated with the eight attributes said to underpin business excellence. Instead, we have offered case reports on the 14 exemplars of excellence that Peters and Waterman (1982) assure us offered beacons for change and renewal within an American economy that had been losing ground to its competitors.

Noting that many have tried and failed to undermine the edifice of the excellence project we have chosen a different approach. While acknowledging the essential truth of those criticisms that have questioned a) the conceptualization of excellence and b) the execution of the methodology employed to gauge corporate conduct we have chosen a different approach. We have considered the lived experience of business excellence and, in so doing, have revealed corporate practices, which Peters and Waterman (1982) somehow failed to consider.

Probing the *real politic* of corporate life and the profane realities of corporate conduct, we have uncovered policies and behaviour that make a mockery of the core *values* said to be central to business excellence. Indeed we have uncovered wholesale misconduct, which suggests the presence of at least a dozen alternative organizational attributes written-out of the excellence project (and cast from the business curriculum). We do not, of course, suggest that every one of the organizations deemed to be exemplary by Peters and Waterman (1982) were criminal and/ or corrupt . . . but some clearly were. Indeed taken as a whole our case reports reveal serious criminality at the heart of those organizations said to exemplify business excellence, namely (1) bribery (2) corruption and (3) money-laundering. Furthermore our case reports have uncovered (4) price-fixing (5) bullying, (6) harassment of staff and stakeholders, (7) racism, (8) anti-Semitism, (9) sexism, (10) false accounting, (11) the falsification of records and (12) double-dealing on a truly industrial scale.

Of course readers may protest that we are – some 40 years after the event – now describing a corporate world that has passed into history. Yet in the face of this anticipated response it is worth reminding ourselves of three things. Firstly, any such attempt to redeem the excellence project simply fails to discharge our central claim. To suggest, therefore, that 'the world is different now' would be to accept the central findings of our inquiry and would, at minimum, acknowledge our contribution to 'business history.' Thus, any attempt to dismiss our analysis as being *merely* historical would be to accept that the exemplars of excellence had, in fact, engaged in conduct which remains truly shocking to this day.

Secondly, the suggestion that our interest in business excellence is merely or narrowly historical must surely be set against the core facts of the argument developed by Peters and Waterman. Thus, it is worth reminding ourselves that *In Search of Excellence* asserted that the exemplary organizations enjoyed economic success because they adhered to a code of values that was truly worthy of celebration. At no point did the authors suggest that their exemplars were mostly decent for their time. At no point did Peters and Waterman (1982) suggest that their excellent organizations were good enough given the broader structural context of their operations. No, the excellent organizations were Peters and Waterman (1982) assured their many readers, good, decent, morally upright and quite unlike other failing organizations *because they had made different and infinitely better moral choices*. Our analysis of course reveals that such claims are simply empty.

Thirdly, while we might like to imagine that things are now different in the organizational world, and while we might hope that, today, the corporations that shape our lives are, law-abiding and have recanted beliefs that were so obviously anti-Semitic and/ or racist and sexist, there is no good reason to presume that our exemplars have, in fact, changed definitively. Therefore, in closing we offer but one example of current misconduct.

In 2019 Delta Airlines, agreed an out-of-court settlement to address the concerns of those passengers who complained that they had suffered losses due to a price-fixing agreement. This agreement, it was alleged, had been brokered among leading players within the industry including Southwest and American Airlines.[18] Evidence of this recent conspiracy rebukes the assertion that the wholesale misconduct we have uncovered among the exemplars of excellence is somehow *yesterday's news*. Furthermore the presence of Southwest Airlines among Delta's co-conspirators is especially notable because this company has been celebrated by Peters (1994; Freiberg and Freiberg, [1996]1998) in more recent iterations of the excellence project for (*ahem*) its obsessive devotion to customers.

In our final chapter we will offer further reflections on the excellence project and upon the business curriculum that has rejected its empirical claims and yet endorsed its central *conceit*.

Notes

1 Peters of course has since altered his position on the merits of Drucker's contribution. Indeed he now publicly celebrates Drucker's insight and legacy (see Collins, 2022).

2 This is an allusion to the conduct of Admiral Horatio Nelson. It is said that during the Battle of Copenhagen, Nelson ignored a direct order (communicated ship-to-ship using flags) to end the action and to retreat. When warned of this signal and order, Nelson is said to have held a telescope to his blind eye (a legacy of an encounter at Cadiz) to announce, truthfully enough, that he could see no ship. Fun fact: Tom Peters is, publicly, a great admirer of Nelson's leadership qualities and practices.

3 As we shall see it might be more accurate to suggest that such figures are reputed rather than reported!

4 This is an addition engineered to remind the reader of Bechtel's anti-Semitism.

5 Pelletier notes that the company established in 1916 was limited by shares. William Boeing held 998 of the 1000 shares issued with his partners sharing the remainder.

6 The company's official rendering of its history, which offers a decade-by-decade account of the company's fortunes and yearly highlights may be found at www.caterpillar.com/en/company/history.html

7 This information is derived from the *Wikipedia* page devoted to *Holt*.

8 There appears to be an error in the account developed by Woolfson and Foster (1988). They suggest that the Caterpillar Tractor Company was founded in 1927, whereas all of the other sources consulted agree on 1925!

9 While on-line sources are often viewed sceptically – and for very good reason – it may be useful to observed that the company histories site draws heavily upon

the *The International Directory of Company Histories,* which is published by St James Press and might, therefore, be taken to be more reliable than most.

10   see https:///www.company-histories.com/Dana-Corporation-History.html

11   Leaving aside refinements in software which in themselves improve the efficiency of computing technology, Moore's Law suggests that the raw processing power of the silicon chips which power our digital devices will continue to double every 18 months.

12   This suggestion builds upon a reading of the discourse of enterprise, developed by the Thatcher governments of the 1980s, which suggested that Britain had lost its enterprising spirit and that the necessary goal of rekindling enterprise would require a new disciplinary matrix that would wean the working class (particularly that proportion located in Scotland) from its supposed dependency on welfare.

13   see www.weitzlux.com

14   Love (1986: 30) demonstrates this unthinking celebration of all things business and management in a number of ways. He avers, for example, that Ray Kroc is 'a legend,' and in a strictly narrative sense, he may now have legendary status. Yet, it is clear that Love employs this epithet to suggest that Kroc is special, great; simply awesome. The problem being that in making this declaration Love chooses to place Kroc in the company of others whom critical historians have often judged more harshly. Thus, Love suggests that Kroc – the legend – is on a par with other titans of business industry such as JD Rockefeller, Andrew Carnegie and Henry Ford and should be given a place in corporate history with these men!

15   The documentary elements of this discussion are drawn from www.3m.com and from www.company-histories.com/3m-company-company-history.html

16   see www.3m.com

17   Due to the choices made by the person(s) compiling the index for *In Search of Excellence,* there is some tension between our calculations and the raw figures revealed by a cursory examination of the index. Digital Equipment Corporation, for example, appears 15 times in the index but there is some level of duplication here such that there are, in truth, just 14 discrete entries on the *Digital Equipment Corporation.* Similarly, there are six mentions of *Fluor* in the index but closer analysis reveals some overlap such that there are, truthfully, just five discrete references to the company in the index.

18   See www.classaction.org/airline-ticket-lawsuit

4 Conclusion

The Emptiness of Business Excellence

This book has been produced to coincide with the 40th anniversary of the first publication of *In Search of Excellence*. We have chosen to mark this 40th anniversary because we understand that *In Search of Excellence* is a very significant work that has contributed to the field of management studies in a number of important ways. *In Search of Excellence* has had a deep and enduring influence on the manner in which we think about management. Furthermore, it has altered the manner in which we talk about management, *and* it has changed quite profoundly the forms of conduct that each of us must undertake in order to demonstrate that we are, in fact, managing in a fashion that is not only productive but commendable. Beyond this impact on practice, however, *In Search of Excellence* remains a commercial phenomenon in its own right. Tom Peters and Robert Waterman have sold millions of copies of their text across the globe. Yet, *In Search of Excellence* has a commercial significance beyond its own astronomical sales because this text, in effect, launched the billion dollar business that is 'popular management.' Indeed the book that so preoccupies us is now generally accepted to be the prototype that became the very archetype of 'popular management' (see Collins, 2021, 2022).

In this book, we have charted the development of *In Search of Excellence* and its success, both as a commercial endeavour and as an enduring commentary on the business of management itself. In chapter two, we considered *In Search of Excellence* in theory. Thus, chapter two offered reflections on the constitution of the argument underpinning *In Search of Excellence*. In addition chapter two considered key criticisms voiced against the excellence project. These critiques, of course, demonstrate that *In Search of Excellence* is, in social scientific terms, a very deeply flawed endeavour that collapses under the weight of its own key claims. And yet, the core message of the excellence project continues to prevail. Indeed we have suggested that the key tenets of *In Search of Excellence* – that managers should be close to the customer, should develop processes that balance

DOI: 10.4324/9781003341086-4

the need for control with the need for autonomy and enterprise, and should lead from the front in a manner that demonstrates commitment to a core set of guiding values – have become so widely accept that they now constitute, in effect, the *lingua franca* of management studies.

Offering reflections designed to explore just why an analysis that is so flawed, scientifically remains so persuasive we have suggested that *In Search of Excellence* has become the touchstone for managerial practice because of its rhetorical construction. Following the analyses developed by Pattison (1997) and Huczynski (1993) among others, we have suggested that *In Search of Excellence* orders and sustains our appreciation of what it, now, means to manage *well* because, even in the absence of a visible deity (or indeed the promise of an after-life), the text offers the affirmation that those committed to business excellence will enjoy conspicuous success and yet remain on the side of the angels.

There is, of course, much to recommend this rhetorical analysis. Indeed it is worth noting that this line of argument usefully rejects the suggestion that managerial practitioners are somehow dopy and/ or have been duped by Peters and Waterman (see Collins, 2001). And yet, we have argued that these rhetorical forms of analysis do not go quite far enough. Indeed we have suggested that the analytical approaches developed by Huczynski (1993) and by Pattison (1997) remain limiting because they fail to consider the larger politics of managerial endeavour, and in so doing, fail to fully understand the *real politic* of corporate life. Thus, while Huczynski (1993) usefully reminds us that managerial work builds and depends upon a core of rhetorical projections, deployed to secure organizational goals and individual ambitions, he does tend to assume that such projects remain bounded by values that are not only lawful but decent.[1] Therefore, in Huczynski's analysis managers are assumed to be always ambitious and, sometimes perhaps, a little vain but they are not generally inclined to prejudice; they would not stoop to discrimination and are, most certainly, neither venal nor criminal.However, analysis of the conduct of those organizations celebrated as exemplars of excellence has revealed a rather different picture.

In our attempt to offer a review of *In Search of Excellence* that is timely, usefully critical, and so, distinctive,[2] we have chosen to address the excellence project at its strongest point. Recognizing the stratified nature of the panel created by Peters and Waterman (1982), we have selected, for analysis, those 14 notable American organizations said to be 'exemplary.' Developing case reports on these 14 organizations we have shown that Peters and Waterman (1982) have developed an account of the business of management which largely ignores 'context[3],' and in so doing, fails to probe conduct within these locales. To remedy this oversight we have set to one side the familiar and conventional critiques and have instead built our case reports on the lived experience of business excellence and upon a consideration of its fifth attribute. Thus, while not blind to the suggestion that the exemplars of excellence would need to be, for example, 'close to the customer' and might choose to 'stick to the knitting' when considering market opportunities, we have concluded that the key test for the exemplars of excellence turns upon the extent to which they are – in a manner that may be voiced in public – 'hands-on; value-driven.'

Given the four decades that have elapsed between the publication of *In Search of Excellence* and our review, we cannot hope to vouch for the extent to which the exemplary organizations were truly characterized by a hands-on managerial approach in the late 1970s. Indeed, we would do well to note that the 'hands-on' concept of management is altogether more complex than is often imagined and hence infinitely variable in its meaning and effects! However, we have been able to consider the values, the practices, preferences and orientations of the excellent organizations. Analysing contemporary reports on the managerial practices of those 14 organizations said to be 'exemplary' we have uncovered evidence of racism, sexism, anti-Semitism, bullying, harassment, bribery, price-fixing, false accounting, corruption, money laundering and – last but not least – unsafe working practices. In other words our reflections on the exemplars of the excellence project reveal not shining beacons of managerial leadership but a full-house on the bingo card of managerial malpractice!

Does this matter now? Does the historical conduct of 14 US organizations selected for analysis in the late 1970s and vaunted in 1982 really matter today?

Our response is straightforward and is, of course, implicit in our introductory chapter and in the remarks that shaped the concluding portion of chapter three. To be clear: the historical conduct of the 'exemplary' organizations matters *here and now* because for 40 years we have been led to believe that the most successful US organizations have maintained a core set of beliefs that rewards performance, values meritocracy and, in so doing, offers meaningful prospects for personal development and societal change. Our review however contradicts this. Indeed we have demonstrated that *In Search of Excellence* actually celebrates organizations which have engaged in forms of conduct that would shame the Russian mafia! Yet our discontent with the exemplary organizations extends beyond the covers of *In Search of Excellence*.

More observant readers will have noted that the core criticisms, which we offered on the theory of business excellence emanate from within the academy. This is as it should be of course. Yet, in seeking a more critical engagement with the practices of the 'exemplary' organizations, and with the lived experience of business excellence, we have been obliged to look beyond the academy and have turned, instead, to those engaged in the trade of journalism. Given this experience we suggest that our review of *In Search of Excellence* might be taken as a prompt to reconsider the excellence project *and* the essential elements of the management curriculum.

Within the UK context there is now a great emphasis on 'impactful'[4] research and on the associated development of forms of learning that are both (somehow) 'real' and 'applied to real life.' And yet this, so-called, 'real life learning' remains blind to the *real politic* of corporate life. We ask: how can a curriculum be 'real' and 'applied' to 'real life' if it chooses simply to ignore practices that, while they are plainly lamentable, are nonetheless present in many organizations and indeed prevalent in some?

We do not really expect an answer to what is, after all, a rhetorical question. Yet for the avoidance of doubt it is worth noting that our review of *In Search of Excellence* demonstrates the existence of a netherworld of management that is, either, unknown within business schools or, where present, is taken to be marginal to the practical endeavours of management, and so, largely irrelevant to the core curriculum.[5] Within an educational agenda driven, ostensibly, by 'impact' and by 'application to real-life problems,' this peculiar constitution of 'mainstream' concerns is by any calculation, nonsensical.

In articulating our discontent with the orthodox, or mainstream curriculum we are not about to advocate forms of scholarly engagement that teach how to bribe, cheat, discriminate and, more broadly, to corrupt. But we cannot continue to protest that our educational process is, either, liberal (in the British sense of the term) or applied to real life (in the manner preferred by the *Department for Education*) so long as we continue to ignore what our analysis has made plain: that individuals and groups will do *and have done* quite terrible things in the pursuit of shareholder value.

George Orwell [1966] (1988) once quipped that biographies may be trusted as faithful only if they reveal something disgraceful about the subject.[6] Accepting this as a meaningful watermark for our endeavours we have developed, for the first time within the academy, genuinely faithful biographies of the exemplars of business excellence. Indeed in revealing truly disgraceful forms of misconduct across the 14 exemplars of excellence we have, while recognizing the influence and importance of *In Search of Excellence*, demonstrated surely its true and lasting legacy: the triumph of faith over facts and the shallow pretence that those who steward our corporations subscribe to a core set of values that is genuinely worthy of public acclaim.

Having revealed truly monumental levels of misconduct amongst those organizations taken to be the best and, apparently, the most wholesome in the US economy, the challenge for business schools, we suggest, is to locate this appreciation of the *real politic* of corporate endeavour *within* the curriculum *without* palming it off to colleagues who teach 'ethics.' Indeed the challenge is to let our analytical description of widespread misconduct speak loudly, and for itself, while avoiding the headlong rush to place new, empty, prescriptions on students and practitioners.[7]

In closing it may be useful to observe that in our attempt to rethink the lived experience of business excellence and the broader legacy of the excellence project we have focused our attention, largely, on the 1960s, the 1970s and the early 1980s. For the most part we have avoided the discussion of more contemporary events and processes because we have been keen to explore what Peters and Waterman (1982) *might* have known and *should have shared* about their exemplars. For the moment we will leave it to others to essay a more contemporary understanding of the realities of corporate life. Yet, as we take a step back from this issue we suggest that it is time for the academy of management to step forward. Indeed in closing we suggest that the academy of management must now reconsider the problematics of its curriculum and in so doing must recognize that any commitment to 'relevance' and 'real-life' learning must require that it stops out-sourcing its conscience.

Notes

1 Here we quite deliberately invoke a term, much used by George Orwell. Orwell's notion of decency is a secular one and is, of course, very much tied up with ideas such as compassion, honesty, freedom and respect for human life. Viewed in these terms many of the exemplary organizations simply lack those characteristics of conduct that Orwell (or indeed any other sentient person) would consider to be 'decent.'

2 While the academy has spent rather a lot of time lambasting practitioners for their pursuit of innovations that are said to be 'faddish' the reality is that academic narratives, if they are to be successful, must turn upon two hinges: currency and controversy. In this regard novelty is, in fact, very highly prized within academic circles, hence the need for our account to be distinctive!

3 Following Pettigrew (1985) the concept of 'context' has a temporal dimension, and so, includes a consideration of history.

4 A hateful, highly ambiguous, and so, deeply political neologism!

5 The experience of those 'critical' academics deemed superfluous to Leicester University's drive to become more 'mainstream' offers a rather worrying indication of what are now taken to be legitimate research concerns and indeed practical forms of pedagogy within the domain of management studies.

6 We have stretched things just a little. Truthfully Orwell's concern relates to the self-serving nature of *autobiographies*. Given the lack of balance and the clear absence of any broader objectivity within the excellence project the distinction is hardly significant for our present purposes.

7 At the peak of the global financial crisis that enveloped us in 2008 some comedian (we can only assume that the initiative was intended as a joke) suggested that *Harvard Business School* was considering requiring its graduates to swear what

amounted to a Hippocratic Oath for management on graduation day. There are at least three problems (and probably many more besides) with this suggestion of oath-taking within management. Firstly the oath would have no meaningful effect since there is no college of practitioners (equivalent to those operating within law and medicine for example) that could exclude recalcitrant general managers from this field of practice. Secondly, the oath would deal with organizationally systemic issues by placing duties on individuals and the world is littered with the broken corpses of whistleblowers who have been crushed by the weight of corporate politics. Thirdly, the misconduct we have uncovered is not currently difficult to manage or to police and does not require new layers of regulation. In short there is no need for a voluntary oath (whether couched as a joke or otherwise) to address forms of conduct that so obviously transgress civil codes, criminal statutes and more elemental forms of human decency.

Bibliography

Ackman D (2002) 'Excellence Sought – And Found,' *Forbes*. www.forbes.com/2002/10/10/1004excellent.html

Aupperle K E, Acar W and Booth D E (1986) 'An Empirical Critique of *In Search of Excellence*: How Excellent are the Excellent Companies?,' *Journal of Management*, 12 (4): 499–512.

Barnard C I [1938] (1968) *The Functions of the Executive*, Harvard University Press, Boston MA.

Baskerville S and Willett R (eds) (1985) *Nothing Else to Fear: New Perspectives on America in the Thirties*, Manchester University Press, Manchester.

Bennis W (2009) *On Becoming a Leader*, Addison-Wesley: New York NY.

Berlin R K (1986) 'Rene McPherson Inducted to Business Hall of Fame,' *Fortune* 14/04/ 1986.

Black E (2001) *IBM and the Holocaust: The strategic Alliance between Nazi Germany and America's most powerful corporation*, Little Brown and Company, London.

Bogner W C (2002) 'Tom Peters on the Real World of Business,' *Academy of Management Executive*, 16 (1): 40–44.

Boltanski L and Chiapello E (2007) *The New Spirit of Capitalism*, trans. Gregory Elliot. Verso, London.

Burrell G (1997) *Pandemonium*, Sage, London.

Business Week (5/11/1984) 'Who's Excellent Now?': 46–54.

Byrne J A (1992) 'Ever in Search of a New Take on Excellence,' *Business Week*, 31/08/1992.

Byrne J A (2001) 'The Real Confessions of Tom Peters,' *Business Week* 12/03/2001.

Carroll D T (1983) 'A Disappointing Search for Excellence,' *Harvard Business Review*, Nov–Dec: 78–82

'Caterpillar tries to dig itself out,' *Los Angeles Times*, 13/01/1985.

Clayman M (1987) 'In Search of Excellence: The Investor's Viewpoint,' *Financial Analysts Journal*, May–June: 54–63.

Collins D (1998) *Organizational Change: Sociological Perspectives*, Routledge, London and New York, NY.

Collins D (2000) *Management Fads and Buzzwords: Critical-Practical Perspectives*, Routledge, London and New York, NY.

Collins D (2001) 'The Fad Motif in Management Scholarship,' *Employee Relations*, 23 (1): 26–37.

Collins D (2007) *Narrating the Management Guru: In Search of Tom Peters*, Routledge, London and New York, NY.

Collins D (2008) 'Has Tom Peters Lost the Plot? A Timely Review of a Celebrated Management Guru,' *Journal of organizational Change Management*, 21 (3): 315–334.

Collins D (2013) 'In Search of Popular Management: Sensemaking, Sensegiving and Storytelling in the Excellence Project,' *Culture and Organization* 19 (1): 42–61.

Collins D (2018) *Stories for Management Success: The Power of Talk in Organizations*, Taylor and Francis, Routledge, London and New York, NY.

Collins D (2021) *Management Gurus: A Research Overview*, Taylor and Francis, Routledge, London and New York, NY.

Collins D (2022) *Tom Peters and Management: A History of Organizational Storytelling*, Taylor and Francis, London and New York, NY.

Collins J (2001) *Good to Great: Why Some Companies Make the Leap and Others Don't*, Random House, London.

Collins J and Porras J I [1994] (2004) *Built to Last: Successful Habits of Visionary Companies*, Random House, London.

Covey S [1989] (2020) *The 7 Habits of Highly Effective People: Powerful Lessons in Personal Change*, Simon and Schuster, London.

Crainer S (1997) *Corporate Man to Corporate Skunk: The Tom Peters Phenomenon, A Biography*, Capstone, Oxford.

DeLamarter R T [1986] (1988) *Big Blue: IBM's Use and Abuse of Power*, Pan Books, London.

Denton S (2016) *The Profiteers: Bechtel and the Men Who Built the World*, Simon and Schuster, New York, NY.

Du Gay P (2000) *In Praise of Bureaucracy*, Sage, London.

The Economist, 08/05/1981.

Freiberg K and Freiberg J [1996] (1998) *NUTS! Southwest Airline's Crazy Recipe for Business and Personal Success*, Orion Business Books, London.

Fukuda J (1988) *Japanese-Style Management Transferred: The Experience of East Asia*, Routledge, London.

Fukuyama F (1992) *The End of History and the Last Man*, Free Press, New York, NY.

Geneen H S with Moscow A (1986) *Managing*, Grafton Books, London.

Geertz C (1993) *The Interpretation of Cultures*, Fontana, London.

Gibbs R K (2020) *Hewlett-Packard and Xerox: The Story of Two American Icons*, Self-Published.

Guest D (1992) 'Right Enough to be Dangerously Wrong: An Analysis of the *In Search of Excellence* Phenomenon,' in Salaman G (ed) *Human Resource Strategies*, Sage, London.

Hayes T C (1979) 'Dana: Few Rules, Many Sales,' *New York*, NY *Times*, 19/10/1979

Hayes R H and Abernathy W J (1980) 'Managing our Way to Economic Decline,' *Harvard Business Review*, July–August: 67–77.

Heller R [1994] (1995) *The Fate of IBM*, Warner Books, London.

Heller R (2000) *Tom Peters: The Bestselling Prophet of the Management Revolution*, Dorling Kindersley, London.

Hilmer F and Donaldson L (1996) *Management Redeemed: Debunking the Fads that Undermine Our Corporations*, Free Press, New York, NY.

Huczynski A A (1993) *Management Gurus: What Makes Them and How to Become One*, Routledge, London.

Hyatt J (1999) 'When Everyone Was Excellent,' *Inc.com*. http://pf.inc.com/magazine/19990515/4703.html

Jackson N and Carter P (1998) 'Management Gurus: What Are We to Make of Them?' in Hassard J and Holliday R (eds) *Organization-Representation: Work and Organization in Popular Culture*, Sage, London.

Jensen M C (1975) 'How 3M Got Tangled Up in Politics,' *The New York Times*, 09/03/1975.

Kahn H (1970) *The Emerging Japanese Superstate*, Harper and Row, London.

Kahn H and Pepper T (1978) *The Japanese Challenge: The Success and Failure of Economic Success*, Harper and Row, London.

Kauffman L A (1993) 'Democracy Is in the Suites,' *The Nation*, 256 (20): 712–713.

Kiechel W (2010) *The Lords of Strategy: The Secret Intellectual History of The new Corporate World*, Harvard Business Review Press, Boston, MA.

Knight C with Dyer D (2005) *Performance without Compromise: How Emerson Consistently Achieves Winning Results*, Harvard Business School Press, Boston, MA.

Kroeber A L and Kluckhohn C (1952) *Culture: A Critical Review of Human Culture – the History of Human Culture, Its Role in Social Science*, Reprinted by Pantianos Classics.

Kropotkin P (1906) *The Conquest of Bread*, Chapman Hall, London.

Latour B (1987) *Science in Action*, Harvard University Press, Cambridge, MA.

'Law-suits, pay-outs and opioids crises: What happened to Johnson & Johnson?' *The Guardian*, 18/10/2019.

Lewis W D and Newton W P [1979] (2016) *Delta: The History of an Airline*, University of Georgia Press, Georgia.

Lischinsky A (2008) 'Examples as Persuasive Argument in Popular Management Literature,' *Discourse and Communication*, 2 (3): 243–269.

Love J F (1986) *McDonald's: Behind the Arches*, Bantam Books, New York, NY.

Maidique M A (1983) 'Point of View: The New Management Thinkers,' *California Management Review*, 26 (1): 151–161.

McCartney L (1988) *Friends in High Places: The Bechtel Story: The Most Secret Corporation and How It Engineered the World*, Simon and Schuster, London.

McDonald D [2013] (2020) *The Firm: The World's Most Controversial Management Consultancy*, OneWorld Publications, London.

Mitchell T R (1985) 'In Search of Excellence versus the 100 Best Companies to Work for in America: A Question of Perspective and Values,' *The Academy of Management Review*, 10 (2): 350–355.

New York Times, 16/07/1969.

New York Times, 25/01/1970.

New York Times, 10/03/1976.

New York Times, 11/02/1979.

New York Times, 28/08/1979.

New York Times, 11/09/1979.

New York Times, 15/12/2018.

New York Times, 20/12/2018.

New York Times, 29/10/2019.

Orwell G [1966] (1988) 'Benefit of Clergy: Notes on Salvador Dali,' in *Decline of the English Murder and Other Essays*, Penguin, Harmondsworth Middlesex.

Packard D (1995) *The HP Way: How Bill Hewlett and I Built Our Company*, Kirby D and Lewis K (eds) Harper Business, New York, NY.

Pascale R T and Athos A G [1981] (1986) *The Art of Japanese Management*, Sidgwick and Jackson, London.

Pastides H, Calabrese E J, Hosmer Jr D W and Harris D R (1988) 'Spontaneous Abortion and General Illness Symptoms Among Semiconductor Manufacturers,' *Journal of Occupational Medicine*, 30 (7): 543–551.

Pattison S (1997) *The Faith of the Managers: When Management Becomes Religion*, Cassell, London.

Pelletier A [2008] (2010) *Boeing: The Complete Story*, Haynes Publishing, Yeovil, Somerset.

Peters T (1994) *The Pursuit of Wow: Every Person's Guide to Topsy-Turvy Times*, MacMillan, London.

Peters T (2018) *The Excellence Dividend: Meeting the Tech Tide with Work that Wows and Jobs that Last*, Vintage, New York, NY.

Peters T (2001a) *In Search of Excellence: A Three-Generation Report Card*, Tom Peters Company, New York, NY.

Peters T (2001b) 'Tom Peters's True Confessions,' *Fast Company*, 53. www.fastcompany.com/magazine/53/peters.html

Peters T and Austin N (1985) *A Passion for Excellence: The Leadership Difference*, London, Fontana.

Peters T and Waterman R (1982) *In Search of Excellence: Lessons from America's Best Run Companies*, Harper and Row, New York, NY.

Pettigrew A (1985) *The Awakening Giant: Continuity and Change in ICI*, Blackwell, Oxford.

Rosenzweig P (2007) *The Halo Effect and Eight Other Business Delusions that Deceive Managers*, Free Press, New York, NY.

Rosner B (2000) 'Tom Peters Sounds Off,' *Workforce*, 56: 58–61.

Sampson A (1973) *The Sovereign State: The Secret History of ITT*, Hodder and Stoughton, London.

Sampson A (1977) *The Arms Bazaar: From Lebanon to Lockheed*, Viking, London.

Saunders J and Wong V (1985) 'In Search of Excellence in the UK,' *Journal of Marketing Management*, 1: 119–137.

Schein E with DeLisi P S, Kampas P J and Sonduck M M (2003) *DEC Is Dead, Long Live DEC: The Lasting Legacy of Digital Equipment Corporation*, Berrett-Koehler Publishers, San Francisco, CA.

Schenker M B , Gold EB, Beaumont J J et al. (1995) 'Association of Spontaneous Abortion and Other Reproductive Effects with Work in the Semiconductor Workers Industry,' *American Journal of Industrial Medicine*, 28: 639–659.

Schoenberg R J (1985) *Geneen*, W W Norton and Co, New York, NY and London.

Selko A (2013) 'How Caterpillar Succeeds,' *Industry Week*, 26/11/2013.

Simpson C (2017) *Business Week*, 15/06/2017.

Sloan A P, McDonald J and Stevens C [1964] (1996) *My Years with General Motors*, Doubleday and Company, New York, NY.

Stewart M [2009] (2010) *The Modern Management Myth: Debunking Modern Business Philosophy*, Norton Paperbacks, London and New York, NY.

Swasy A (1993) *Soap Opera: The Inside Story of Procter and Gamble*, Simon and Schuster, New York, NY.

Van der Merwe R and Pitt L (2003) 'Are Excellent Companies Ethical? Evidence from an Industrial Setting,' *Corporate Reputation Review*, 5 (4): 343–355.

Vine T (2020) *Bureaucracy: A Key Idea for Business and Society*, Taylor and Francis, Routledge, London.

Waterman R, Peters T and Phillips J (1980) 'Structure Is Not Organization,' *Business Horizons*, 23 (3): 14–26.

Watson T (2001) *In Search of Management: Culture, Chaos and Control in Managerial Work*, Thomson Learning, London.

Watson T J [1963] (2003) *A Business and Its Beliefs: The Ideas that Helped Build IBM*, McGraw-Hill, London.

Woolfson C and Foster J (1988) *Track Record: The Story of the Caterpillar Occupation*, Verso, London and New York, NY.

Index

Note: Tables are denoted with **bold** page numbers. End note information is denoted by n and note number following the page number.